T0265479

Praise for *Thinking Bigger*

"From the first sentence, I couldn't put this book down and found myself compelled to share it with all women founders worldwide. Sarah is your pitch 'Super Coach,' sharing personal key tips and tactics that work so that you can pitch authentically and effectively when fundraising!"
　　—Anne Ravanona, founder and CEO, Global Invest Her and Invest Her Summit

"Sarah knocks it out of the park with this much needed book! It is a must read for women entrepreneurs who want to unlock the secrets of how to access venture capital and successfully scale your business."
　　—Catherine Gray, producer, *Show Her the Money*; CEO, She Angel Investors; and host, *Invest in Her* podcast

"In her captivating book, Sarah offers a compelling account of entrepreneurship, weaving together her personal experiences with invaluable lessons for aspiring business leaders. Her insights are particularly poignant for women navigating a male-dominated industry."
　　—Camille Burns, CEO, Women Presidents Organization

"A primer for women entrepreneurs that is both inspirational and a how-to guide. Sarah admits the real challenges of starting and growing a thriving company while also conveying the criticality of mindset and what steps to take to scale successfully. All founders should read this book."
　　—Lisa Schiffman, founder, EY Entrepreneurial Winning Women™, retired director, Ernst & Young LLP

"Dusek provides clear examples and tips to execute on the very first step to get venture capital: the pitch deck."
　　—Alicia Castillo Holley, general partner, Wealthing VC Fund; CEO and founder, Wealthing VC Club; and senior adviser, CEA Group

"*Thinking Bigger* is a must read for women who are building businesses and thinking about raising venture capital. Dusek draws on her experience as an entrepreneur and venture investor to provide incredibly practical and tactical advice to founders who want to scale. A strong pitch deck is critical to attracting capital, and this book is an invaluable guide to creating one."

—Tahira Dosani, managing partner, ResilienceVC

"I wish that I'd had this book to guide and inspire me when I started my entrepreneurial journey. It's a gift to learn from a successful woman entrepreneur who's accessed capital to scale multiple companies."

—Carrie Rich, CEO, The Global Good Fund

"Relatable and easy to read, *Thinking Bigger* offers golden nuggets of wisdom to entrepreneurs from Dusek's own mistakes, revelations, and accomplishments as she built her $100M business."

—Victoria Pettibone, chief investment officer, Astia

"Sarah's story is one of inspiration, grit, and determination and is sure to resonate powerfully with other women who are striving to leverage their entrepreneurial passion in order to make a meaningful difference in the world. A clear and practical roadmap for making your dreams a reality in business and beyond."

—Sheldon Harris, former president, Cold Stone Creamery, partner, CEO
    Coaching International

"A masterclass in entrepreneurship for women underserved by venture capital. Sarah's journey in venture fund creation delivers unmatched insights into securing funding and scaling. More than a book, it's an invaluable mentor in print!"

—Marcia Dawood, SEC adviser, chair emeritus, Angel Capital Association

"Every impact-driven woman entrepreneur needs a motivational voice in her ear, encouraging her to step out of her comfort zone, think bigger, and attract investment. That voice is Sarah Dusek's. If you read one business book this year, make it *Thinking Bigger*—it's your formula for growth and investment success!"

—Melanie Hawkins, founder and CEO, Lionesses of Africa

"Sarah explains the risks that founders are truly taking, how your personal life story shapes your unique advantages and startup ideas, how investors practically evaluate startups, and what a venture-backable startup actually is, shared through the lens of a female (underrepresented) investor, addressing female (underrepresented) founders."

—Olga Duka, GP, Improve Ventures

THINKING

BIGGER

FOREWORD BY SUNEERA MADHANI

SARAH DUSEK

THINKING

BIGGER

A PITCH-DECK FORMULA FOR WOMEN WHO WANT TO CHANGE THE WORLD

Georgetown University Press
Washington, DC

The publisher is not responsible for third-party websites or their content. URL links were active at time of publication.

Library of Congress Cataloging-in-Publication Data

Names: Dusek, Sarah, author.
Title: Thinking bigger : a pitch-deck formula for women who want to change the world / Sarah Dusek.
Description: Washington, DC : Georgetown University Press, 2024. | Includes bibliographical references and index.
Identifiers: LCCN 2024011595 (print) | LCCN 2024011596 (ebook) | ISBN 9781647125080 (hardcover) | ISBN 9781647125097 (ebook)
Subjects: LCSH: New business enterprises—Finance. | Entrepreneurship. | Success in business. | Venture capital. | Businesswomen.
Classification: LCC HG4027.6 .D87 2024 (print) | LCC HG4027.6 (ebook) | DDC 658.15/5—dc23/eng/20240515
LC record available at https://lccn.loc.gov/2024011595
LC ebook record available at https://lccn.loc.gov/2024011596

∞ This paper meets the requirements of ANSI/NISO Z39.48-1992 (Permanence of Paper).

25 24   9 8 7 6 5 4 3 2   First printing

Printed in the United States of America

Cover design by Molly von Borstel, Faceout Studio
Appendix design by Mike Munt, Apogii, UK
Interior design by Robert Kern, TIPS Publishing Services, Carrboro, NC

To every woman who dares to imagine what might be possible.

This book is dedicated to you.

Contents

Foreword

When I first came up with the idea for Stax Payments, I didn't know that I was capable of building a million-dollar business, let alone a billion-dollar business. My first step was to pitch the idea to my boss, who dismissed it. I then reached out to twelve other banks and payment processors, all of whom also turned me down. It never occurred to me that I could take my own idea and run with it without the support of the big players in the finance industry. After all, it's hard to imagine doing something when no one who looks like you is doing something similar. I didn't see any other women of color leading multi-million-dollar enterprises—especially in the fintech field. It wasn't until my immigrant father finally said to me, "Why are you giving this away? Why do you need anyone else?" that I realized I should take charge of my idea. His confidence in me boosted my belief that I should and could take my idea and turn it into something extraordinary. Over the last decade Stax Payments has become one of America's top ten fastest growing fintech companies with a recent valuation of over $1 billion dollars. I know firsthand how challenging it was to make that happen and how many mistakes I made along the way. I understand too few women are taking on the same challenges I did and making remarkable things happen. That's why I am a passionate advocate for women in business, and I am proud to introduce Sarah Dusek's book to you.

I first met Sarah in 2020 when she shared her remarkable dedication to investing in and championing underrepresented female founders in Africa. Listening to her tales of empowering African women to build big businesses and raise venture capital ignited a desire within me to personally connect with some of them. Since then, several of these inspiring women have joined me on my podcast, *The CEO School*, where their stories have had a profound impact on me, much like Sarah's own entrepreneurial journey. It is fascinating to learn how she managed to build an extraordinary pioneering travel company, even with limited capital.

What truly struck me was Sarah's unwavering commitment to making it possible for other women to succeed in their own ventures. Her passion deeply resonates with my belief that empowering women to earn more money and ensuring their presence at the decision-making tables are crucial steps toward building a more equal world. That is why I am immensely honored to recommend this book and introduce Sarah's incredible story to you.

Sarah's journey towards success is truly awe-inspiring, captivating not only just to me but to countless others. Her ascent from a humble start-up to a thriving business owner is truly remarkable. Creating a successful company takes more than a good idea. It demands a unique combination of skills, vision, determination, creativity, resilience, team building, and fundraising. Witnessing another entrepreneur navigate the rollercoaster ride of building a business can help us all understand what it takes to triumph.

As an entrepreneur myself, I intimately understand the challenges that come with building a successful business from scratch. From the day-to-day operational challenges, to securing that pivotal first big "yes" and raising capital, every step of the journey is filled with obstacles. Sarah had a vision to create something that would make a lasting impact in the world, and she faced numerous challenges head-on. She immersed herself in the rules of entrepreneurship, often enduring costly lessons.

What I love about this book is that it seeks to help you avoid making the same mistakes Sarah and I made. It provides the knowledge she wished she had, giving you a leg up. Designed as a guide to propel you further and faster, Sarah shares her insights on the importance of understanding the rules of the game and finding the right people to invest in your extraordinary idea. Sarah knows that with this mindset, the right tools, and grand vision, achieving the impossible becomes possible.

Thinking Bigger aims to disrupt the exclusionary trend where women are sidelined from major capital raises and fail to reach their deserving success. Shockingly, only 18 percent of women reach the six-figure revenue mark, with a mere 2 percent making it to the million-dollar mark. Hence, it's no wonder that we're not getting funded. We are not where we need to be from a revenue standpoint to go and ask for venture capital, and even when we get there, the systems of patriarchy are already stacked against us.

Fortunately, Sarah provides practical insights and invaluable tools that will give you the confidence to elevate your business to the next level and conquer the hurdles that lie ahead. Thanks to Sarah's insights and guidance, we can be better prepared than ever before to think differently and face the challenges and

obstacles along the way. Sarah's openness and honesty in sharing her journey as
a start-up founder reminded me that success is not just about reaching a goal, but
also about the journey we take to get there. I have come to realize that calculated
risks and embracing failures are essential to achieving success. Sarah's courage
in sharing her struggles and setbacks not only reassures us that mistakes are part
of the journey, but in fact they are indispensable in our path to success.

Thinking Bigger is not just a collection of stories. It's a roadmap to success
by Sarah who shares her secrets, tools, and the power of perseverance, growth
mindsets, and relationship building. Success isn't solely determined by hard work;
it hinges on being adaptable and open to learning. Success is attainable, but it
requires shifting our thinking and actions. This book is your guide to not only
thinking bigger but also thinking better. Whether you're a female entrepreneur
or simply someone striving to achieve their goals, Sarah's roadmap will guide
you to success. I wholeheartedly recommend reading *Thinking Bigger* and I am
excited to see where your business will take you with the wisdom and inspiration
that Sarah provides. Let's connect on the other side of success!

—Suneera Madhani, Founder of Stax Payments,
Founder and host of *The CEO School* podcast

Preface

In 2015, six years into building our glamping company, Under Canvas, a venture capitalist (VC) from New York City stayed at one of our luxury camping sites. She loved her stay and our vision of creating extraordinary, tented experiences by making the outdoors accessible to people who wouldn't necessarily ever consider going camping.

"You need to raise capital as soon as possible so you can grow exponentially. I've come across a much less qualified and untested competitor who has raised millions of dollars and is swooping into your industry. If you don't move now, you will lose the market share to this less qualified competitor." This VC was adamant. She spoke of the urgency for us to pitch our vision and business to investors so we could continue to grow in an industry we were already creating and defining.

I loved her advice and the idea of growing our business exponentially, but there was a problem. I had no idea how to raise capital. I didn't even really understand how businesses could be valuable beyond the profit they made annually. The investment arena was vastly different from the world that I navigated at the time. I was concerned with whether we would be able to repay our loans and fulfill our payroll responsibilities and whether we would be profitable. But my conversation with the VC sparked something in me. I instinctively knew that we had an opportunity to do something big and that we were never going to be able to grow fast enough if we only plowed our profits back into the business. Instead, we needed more outside capital to fuel our growth, so the VC explained that I needed a pitch deck so I could pitch investors.

A pitch deck—the standard ten-page formula for communicating with investors—tells a story and shares the data and metrics that matter to VCs. The pitch deck presents the business as a valuable investable commodity and aims to make a lasting impression on its reader in a short amount of time. It is a powerful tool that allows entrepreneurs and business leaders a way of effectively communicating their ideas and potentially securing funding from investors.

Before my encounter with the VC, I had no idea what should be in a pitch deck or what it would take to build a valuable company. Yet the kindness and intention of that one woman forever changed the playing field for me. Learning the rules of the finance game changed how I thought about business; it also changed how I played, and it enabled me to build a business that would become worth more than $100 million and become a VC myself, investing in other women hoping to grow and scale their businesses.

I wrote this book after years of investing in and working with other ambitious female entrepreneurs who, just like me, were not lacking talent but were lacking critical practical knowledge. In my early entrepreneurial days, I had so little understanding of what it would take to build a large business and how to attract funding. Since becoming an investor, I have realized my reality is most women's reality. As an entrepreneur turned venture capitalist, I have come to realize that understanding theory is quite different from applying knowledge in practice. Although you may be familiar with the ten commandments of pitch decks, I have encountered well-educated women who struggle to create compelling pitch decks or effectively communicate the information that truly matters to investors. This book aims to bridge the gap between knowledge and practice, empowering women to secure funding and thrive in big business and finance.

Thinking Bigger is for women entrepreneurs around the world who want to think bigger and understand what it will take to get funded. So many women would love to build something great but don't know the rules of the game. We want real, practical, useable tools to help us make big things happen. In this book, we'll delve into the art and science of creating a winning pitch deck, from crafting a compelling story to using data and design to make a lasting impact. I offer real-life examples from other female entrepreneurs and stories from my own journey both as an entrepreneur and now as an investor in other women's businesses. Whether you are a start-up founder, an entrepreneur, or a business professional, this book aims to give you the tools you need to help you and your business truly stand out and achieve success.

Increasing the number of women-led businesses is not only beneficial for individual women entrepreneurs but is also critical for building a more equal, diverse world. Studies have shown that companies with more diverse leadership tend to perform better financially. But not only is equality good for global economics. The more diversified a business' contributing members are, and the more diversified solution finders are, the healthier our world will be for everyone. Our world is in desperate need of women entrepreneurs who will bring their unique perspectives to solving some of the world's biggest and most stubborn problems. This book is a rallying cry to encourage women to think big, to take their seats at the proverbial tables of power, and to build their own tables if necessary.

Women-led businesses face significant barriers to obtaining funding. Women routinely access less than 2 percent of all venture capital deployed annually—a statistic that's barely changed in over twenty-five years. This book is designed to help women change those statistics by unlocking the keys to capital, which is a critical resource for building something of scale. The capital markets have specific rules—rules that have largely been developed by men, for men—but if more women understand those rules, then we are empowered to either play by the rules, reinvent the rules, or break the rules. Knowledge is power. A pitch deck is more than just the delivery of information about our idea to potential stakeholders; it is the doorway into a world that often excludes women.

This book is designed to be an insider's approach to help women understand the rules around investment funding and realize what makes something investable so that they, too, can make big things happen by harnessing the power of the pitch deck. Each chapter in this book is designed to correlate with the traditional format of the ten-page pitch deck as follows:

1. Title page
2. The problem
3. The solution
4. The product
5. Market size
6. Revenue model
7. Traction
8. Competition
9. Your team
10. Your ask

While there are no hard and fast rules regarding the order of these pages or limits on how many pages you can present in your deck, these ten pages outline the most fundamental information an investor wants to see in your presentation. Each chapter in this book seeks to unpack the content required for each page of the pitch deck and aims to provide strategies and resources for women to effectively communicate their ideas and learn the keys that make scaling and growing a big business possible. In addition to the content required, we will also explore the mindsets that hold women back, seeking to uncover the layers of conditioning that often keep women stymied.

Unfortunately, raising capital and scaling a business does not get easier, even if you have done it before. I foolishly thought after scaling my own company and successfully exiting it that it would be easy to raise capital for my next venture and easy to help other women do what I had done. I was wrong. It turns out that the path continues to be riddled with challenges, obstacles, and frustrations, and the mindsets we each possess are a far more critical component to our success than we might imagine. That is why it is critical to not only learn the information you may not already know but also to unravel the thinking that is getting in your way. This book is designed to be your guide in helping you identify unhelpful thinking that is holding you back.

We will meet several other female entrepreneurs in this book whose stories I am proud to tell alongside my own. Many of them have done or are doing extraordinary things. I hope you will be able to identify yourself in our collective stories and will find yourself caught up as part of an ongoing story of women rising. May this book inspire you to do great things and empower you to build your own big business, create extraordinary impact, drive needed change, and build a more equitable world.

Let's get started.

Questions for Reflection

- What do you believe is currently getting in your way?
- Are you ready to put rocket fuel in your engine and think bigger than ever?
- How might putting additional resources into your business change your trajectory?
- Could you help another woman you know move forward on her journey today?

Slide One of the Pitch Deck: Title Page

Open your pitch presentation with your business name, logo, and tagline if you have one. Show off your unique branding style, create excitement, and entice your audience to learn more.

The Heart of the Problem

It's hard to be what you can't see.

—Marian Wright Edelman

If someone had told me in 2008, "Sarah, in ten years, your company will be worth over 100 million dollars," I would have laughed long and hard. Such a monumental number was so far removed from my reality. Our first foray into business ended in disaster when the Global Economic Crisis of 2008 virtually wiped us out financially. My husband Jake and I had started a socially-minded property development company in 2006 in my native UK, which sought to equip and train young school leavers who were graduating without any qualifications with the practical skills they need. We launched the business to explore whether our work could be a force for good in the world while harnessing the power of enterprise to do environmental and social good. We both had come from a background of working for non-profit organizations whose very existence was based on being able to make the world a better place. Still, many years in the non-governmental organization (NGO) space had left me burned out, disillusioned, and frustrated by the lack of change, as no real big issues were getting solved. Hitting the wall emotionally and mentally meant I had to go back to the drawing board and reimagine my career, rethink my path, and open my mind to other possibilities and realities—something I felt ill-equipped to do. But there is nothing like hitting rock bottom to force you to figure out a way to pick yourself back up.

Expanding my worldview and my thinking about my place in the world was not an easy shift to make, but this was also the moment when I had a big "ah ha" moment. I realized my instinct for making the world a better place was a great driver but that I might not be in the right vehicle for driving innovation, solving problems, and creating solutions to real needs. It dawned on me that non-profit organizations are designed to support, care, assist, and help people in need but that solving big issues and getting to the root of problems isn't in their DNA—but solving problems, innovating, and creating sustainable solutions is in the DNA of a business. That is why any business exists—to solve customer needs, to provide a service, and to innovate solutions to problems in a sustainable way.

Bolstered by our new thinking, Jake and I launched ourselves off on a new endeavor into the world of business. We didn't know anything about running a venture; we had no experience, no business degree, and no money of our own, but plenty of idealism and a deep belief that creating profit and having purpose didn't need to be mutually exclusive. We were sure business had the power to do good—to transform communities, cities, and nations.

However, 2008 rolled around to shatter our dreams, and our endeavors abruptly came to a halt when the bottom fell out of the housing market. This was the biggest financial crash of my lifetime, and it threw the capital markets into disarray. Suddenly, the properties we had bought were worth less after we had renovated them than when we originally bought them in their derelict state. It was a disaster. We had to lay everyone off and face the reality that we had excruciating financial pressure and mounting debts. I was pregnant with our first child, and instead of getting to prepare the nursery for our imminent arrival, we had to move out of our own home and get it rented to tenants to pay the mortgage to prevent our own small home from being repossessed. The world as we knew it was collapsing around us. Feeling we were out of options, we moved in with my parents, and after the arrival of our son we started to contemplate our next steps. Realizing we had to start over yet again, Jake encouraged me to think about picking up our little family and heading to Montana to his family's farm, where he had grown up. He loved the idea of raising a family on the farm, and now nothing (other than a considerable amount of debt) was tying us to the UK. We packed our bags, said teary goodbyes to my family in the UK, and arrived in the US during the summer of 2009, determined to figure out how on earth we were now going to earn a living.

Montana and the family farm afforded our family some physical and mental breathing room. The big, wide-open spaces, huge skies, and cows that outnumbered people gave us both a chance to process all that had happened in the previous few years. Montana also sparked an unexpected idea. Not willing to give up on the idea of starting a business and creating something that could do good, we started over. Reliant on food stamps to feed our small family, with much debt still hanging over us, a baby in tow, and barely two cents to rub together, we got to work thinking about how we could leverage the one asset we did have access to, Jake's family's farm.

In my early twenties, I worked as an aid worker in Zimbabwe and fell in love with the African safari experience. The sheer joy of being out in nature while simultaneously having a comfortable, clean bed, a flushing toilet, and a hot shower was my idea of heaven. When I met and married my husband Jake a few years later, he was, and still is, a big outdoors guy. Coming from Montana, he loved camping, fishing, hiking, and being in the wilderness as much as possible. He didn't mind roughing it. I, on the other hand, had absolutely no intention of sleeping on the ground or digging a hole in the woods to poop in. The mere idea of sleeping on the ground, with no flushing toilets, simply was not appealing. I needed (and still do) running water, a hot shower, and a nice, comfortable bed with plush, clean linens. We had a problem, Houston! But this was a problem that sparked an idea, a spark that ultimately led to the creation of Under Canvas.

Montana is a place that bears similarities to Africa—plenty of wildlife, big prairies, and lots of wild spaces. It dawned on us: what if we could recreate the African safari experience in Montana? Could we build comfortable tents for people to stay out in the wilderness? Could we launch ourselves again into an arena we knew very little about? Could we pick ourselves up and start another business after an initial failure?

The Voice in Our Heads

Impostor syndrome is a pervasive mental obstacle for women in male-dominated fields like finance and big business. Women in male-dominated spaces often feel that they don't belong, don't have the credentials to be there, that they shouldn't, or that they simply can't do it. What we often don't allow for or give ourselves space to recognize, however, is that we still don't belong. We are still having to battle patriarchal discrimination and narratives that undermine our very existence in the workplace.[1] We continue to operate in spaces where women are few and far between and where women are not treated in the same way as men.[2] Lack of female representation often contributes to a persistent fear that somehow, we might be exposed as a fraud or not worthy or that we shouldn't be doing what we are. It's not surprising, therefore, that so many women feel like imposters. Yet, we can't allow our own or society's narratives to keep us playing a small game. We must not allow the defeatist voices in our heads to drown out any belief that we may have what it takes to rise and take our seats at the table. We cannot allow impostor syndrome to sabotage ourselves.

I certainly felt inhibited as we contemplated launching another new venture where neither of us had any experience. Still bearing the scars of our recent failure, I questioned whether Jake was better suited to entrepreneurship and if I should take a back seat. I couldn't imagine what role I could play other than that of the supportive wife, as I had a small child tied to my hip and no previous experience in the hospitality business or any previous business success. Unlike Jake, I didn't have an area where I felt competent. Jake had his construction experience and expertise to fall back on. I felt alone, far from home, and intensely vulnerable. Yet I had learned from years of living overseas as a young woman by myself that anytime I had ever done anything for the first time or had learned something new rapidly, I had felt deeply vulnerable. Somehow, this vulnerability felt familiar, and I realized this was another opportunity to take a leap of faith with this new business idea. We would be exposed again, out on a limb, and going to a destination where no one had quite gone before, but at the same time, I would feel alive, exhilarated, and challenged. I didn't want to miss out on what could possibly be, and so despite feeling inadequate, unqualified, and inexperienced, I chose to silence my fears and embrace my own discomfort. Nothing makes being exposed easier, but we can become more used to the sensation when we realize nothing qualifies or disqualifies us either.

As entrepreneurs, we must acknowledge and address the negative self-talk, the imposter syndrome that often holds us back. By recognizing and countering these self-limiting beliefs, we can unlock possibilities for ourselves and, ultimately, our world. We don't belong in traditional patriarchal environments, but we can create new paths, new possibilities, and new ways forward for ourselves. We can lean into our own vulnerabilities and question marks regarding what is possible. We can choose to believe in ourselves rather than doubt. Instead of seeking to feel like we belong or are good enough for what already exists, we can instead seek to create new possibilities, new pathways where none exist. Although doubt may occasionally creep in, I keep reminding myself, "Why not me? If not me, then who?" Creating new mantras for ourselves that counteract the fear, doubt, and disbelief will be important for each of us as we start to get creative with imagining our futures while acknowledging that the world we currently live in is not set up for us to easily succeed. We will need to surround ourselves with cheerleaders, both real and imagined, who can drown out the negative voices in our minds. Together, we can overcome the constraints of the current world and redefine the rules of success.

Like most women entrepreneurs, I lived outside of the elite club of those with a master's of business administration (MBA), who have learned business principles in school, and who are armed with a network of people in the financial industry. I had not gone to an Ivy League school that had given me lots of impressive connections. Instead, I was forced to make up our business systems and processes as I went. I worked with the limited knowledge and resources I had, which in the early days of our new Montana business meant levering multiple credit cards and frantically juggling balances between cards. But my perceived lack of credentials or resources did not prohibit me from being able to build an extraordinarily valuable big business, and it shouldn't hinder you either. We need to loudly cheer each other on and tell our stories so that the secrets of wealth creation are no longer only for the elite special few. We need more women to know more broadly, "This is what it takes, here's how you get there, this is what happens, and more importantly, this is why you should do it."

Countless products that women founders have developed in the past two decades would never have been created by men; for example, the felt-covered hanger, the tampon, and later the menstrual cup. Underwear that holds your muffin-top in, a mop that can be wrung without getting your hands dirty, and even further back, the dishwasher invented by Josephine Cochrane in 1887; the ice cream freezer invented by Nancy Johnson in 1843; the modern electric refrigerator invented by Florence Parpart in 1914; the most famous board game of all time, Monopoly, invented by Elizabeth Magie in 1904, originally designed to critique the injustices of unchecked capitalism; and the various technological advances from the work of Dr. Shirley Jackson, the first black woman to receive a Ph.D. from the Massachusetts Institute of Technology (MIT) in 1973. While working at Bell Laboratories, Dr. Jackson conducted breakthrough basic scientific research that enabled others to invent the portable fax, the touch-tone telephone, solar cells, fiber optic cables, and the technology behind caller ID and call waiting.

Ideas that women have had and the businesses they have built have shaped our culture and impacted our lives. For this reason, women must lead in the arena of business. Without women of all diverse backgrounds seated at the table in our society, the shaping of our cultures will be limited in the type of products and services that come to market and the industries that develop. If we do not have a diverse pool of founders building businesses, quite simply, too many of the world's problems will go unsolved, and we'll continue to build a world that is not for everyone. The formation and growth of companies are integral to the shaping of society. Women are not only *capable* but *should* make big things happen in our world.

Entrepreneurs are the builders of our world, creating the companies that inform and change our lives. If women routinely do not have a seat at the table of creating and running global corporations—making big things happen—the world we build will continue to serve only a small segment of its population. Without women entrepreneurs, we will perpetuate a world where marginalized populations, particularly women and people of color, are forced to live in a world consciously designed to exclude them.

Too Small

Today, there are not enough women building big companies. In 2020, a couple of years after successfully exiting Under Canvas, I joined an angel investor group in New York City, and I knew every single female founder who pitched that day— every single one of them! I thought, "Something is wrong here. The pool of women seeking funding is way too small."

Not only is the pool too small, but in the role I now play as a venture capitalist investor, I frequently hear pitches from female entrepreneurs in which they project they could get to $1 million of revenue in ten years. I always say, "No, no, no, no, no! The better question is how do you get to $1 million of revenue in your first eighteen months, and how do you get to $100 million in ten years?!" Venture-backed companies, for example, are expected to be in a race against the clock to grow their first $1 million in revenue, or if they are tech companies, exponentially grow their user numbers in their first eighteen months in business.

Each time I have pointed out to a female entrepreneur that she was thinking too small or planning to move too slowly, she has thanked me. She had not realized until that moment that her understanding of *big* was not very big at all. She simply hadn't imagined a world in which she could build a big business or understand the expectation of the need to move fast or what *big* really looks like. For the purposes of this book, I am defining "big" as a company worth $100 million or more since that is what venture capitalists primarily seek. Knowing what is expected of a company that receives capital or that is attempting to scale is half the battle. It is, after all, hard to be what you cannot see or know what the route looks like when you've not seen the roadmap. Women need to start thinking differently about scale, realizing that a business that does $1 million of revenue is not considered big. We need to start where we can imagine, but we then need to multiply that by one hundred times. That might start to get many of us into the right ballpark!

How big are you currently thinking? Are you thinking big enough? Does thinking "$100 million big" scare you? If so, you are not alone. Historically, women have generally been conditioned to think smaller and build slowly based on what they knew or believed they could successfully manage, leaning toward lifestyle businesses rather than building large businesses. The responsibilities of child rearing and home management largely still land firmly on women's shoulders and deeply affect women's capacity and what women imagine is possible. Juggling parenting, being responsible for others' well-being, and aggressively pursuing building something of extraordinary scale is a daunting prospect. Just the other day, a female entrepreneur reached out to me to say, "You challenged me to think bigger and bolder and to fight against the little devil on my shoulder, constantly whispering that being a good mother and scaling a business can't be done at the same time!" That's the thought that many of us live with, that it's impossible to be great mothers if we are playing a big game. We get stuck with outdated thinking regarding what being a good mother looks like or what it will require of us, which might be too costly for our families if we take on huge challenges. We succumb to thoughts that keep us playing a smaller game rather than deciding to find solutions to those very real challenges.

Currently, less than 2 percent of women-owned businesses do more than $1 million in revenue annually.[3] This reinforces the reality that only a very small percentage of women are thinking big. Further, only 2 percent of all venture capital dollars annually goes to fund female entrepreneurs, although this number is slightly higher (17 percent) for mixed-gender founding teams.[4] It is a sad reality that a woman's chances of receiving funding are higher if she has a male cofounder, as I did. Likely, the lack of funding going to women is, in part, due to women not thinking or building big enough but also being largely excluded from what is an almost exclusively boys' financial club. Not having access to capital severely limits what women are capable of building. Fewer than thirty women have taken the companies they founded public on either the National Association of Securities Dealers Automated Quotations (NASDAQ) or New York Stock Exchange (NYSE) in the history of IPOs (Initial Public Offerings).[5] In the almost two-hundred-and-fifty-year history of US stock exchanges, this represents only a handful of women taking a company public. Yet another indicator that women are woefully under-funded as companies that go public typically have become exceptionally valuable, often already being worth well over $1 billion before IPO. Companies that become large and valuable require significant capital to build them. Women need capital if they are going to think big and grow big companies.

I firmly believe that if women know the rules regarding what investors are looking for and expecting to see in a business, and if they see other women not only playing the big business game but also being great mothers and succeeding at building great companies, then more women will be able to think big and build their businesses differently. It's time we become the role models someone else needs to see.

Imagining More

In 2017, the year we finally managed to secure institutional investment into our rapidly growing Montana-based business, I was lucky enough to be drafted into the Ernst & Young Global Limited (EY) Entrepreneurial Winning Women program, which is a bit like the Oscars for entrepreneurs, with a competitive award that recognizes women for the work they've done and the companies they've built. By that time, the program had existed for ten years, and they had selected ten to twelve women each year. Over nearly a decade, the program has recognized over one hundred women with massive dreams. Some went on to sell their companies for hundreds of millions of dollars, some for billions of dollars, some were now venture capitalists investing in other businesses, and others transitioned into local and national politics. For the first time in my entrepreneurial journey, I met other women who were making big things happen—they thought about leading in ways I had never imagined. They weren't just thinking about building one big company; they were thinking about using their resources to advance our world. They were building a platform that would enable them to make the world better. Some were moving into politics and were talking about running for office. Some were building billion-dollar companies. It was revolutionary for me because they were unapologetically thinking big. It set a new precedent for what I'd considered my ceiling and what I thought was possible. My thoughts about what I wanted, what I wanted to do, and even what I *could* do grew exponentially. The scale of what I thought was possible for my life altered dramatically. Suddenly, I could imagine myself building a company worth a billion dollars, building a venture capital firm investing in women, transforming developing continent's gross domestic products (GDPs) by creating access to thoughtful capital, and empowering fledgling entrepreneurs. My thoughts had dramatically shifted from my early thoughts regarding being a sidekick to my husband in his entrepreneurial endeavours and even my current context of being a successful chief executive officer (CEO) of a multi-million-dollar business. Being surrounded by inspiring, powerful women changed my world.

Our time has come, as women, to step out of our comfort zones and start forging roads that have not yet been paved, taking on challenges that look like mountains, and believing that we can overcome every obstacle we will face as we shape the future. We must recognize the boxes we have put ourselves in through our thinking so we can claw our way out. We must recognize that we cannot wait for someone else to step up or have courage but that each of us has a role to play in building our world and solving some of the biggest problems of our time.

Our world is evolving rapidly. Catastrophic weather events and pandemics, not seen for a hundred years, have recently spread across the globe, reminding us of just how fragile our world is. We need women from all backgrounds to contribute solutions to the world's problems; otherwise, we will continue to veer in a direction that creates vaster inequalities and bigger threats to humanity. The proverbial decision-making power tables affect all our futures. With the world's wealth managed by less than 1 percent of the world's population, we will not create a different and better world unless we make fundamental changes in how we operate, how we deploy capital, and how wealth is distributed. Wealth is most certainly power, and a small subsector of white men wield an unfathomable amount of power that dictates how the rest of the world's population lives and behaves. What our world will look like in the next ten, twenty, and one hundred years will largely be determined by those who control the world's wealth and those who access that wealth. Women need to not only be among those building wealth but also become the ones distributing it. Just as women naturally solve different problems than men, women will also deploy capital differently than men, investing in solutions for the problems only we can see through our cultural and gender lenses. Women will envision different possibilities for our world, and potentially contribute to a more inclusive, holistic, sustainable future for us all.

Women, therefore, must step up and say, "We will be funded. We will grow big businesses. We will play our part in changing the way the world looks, feels, smells, and tastes. We will take our seats at the boys' table, or we will create our own table. We will stop thinking we don't deserve to be there or that we can't be there because the world needs us to be there." With women at those tables, there is a chance for a future that doesn't look exactly like our past. With women at the table, we can conceive of an inclusive world for everyone. Will you help build that world?

One Specific Big Problem

The first step in solving the world's big problems is to develop a razor-sharp focus on the one problem that anchors your business idea. What is the fundamental problem your business is aiming to solve? The second slide of the pitch deck always opens (after your impressively designed title cover on slide one) by outlining the specific problem you intend to solve with your business. This is where your story begins, telling investors succinctly and clearly about the problem you intend to solve and why that matters. This is your opening punch that gives investors an indicator to determine if you are solving a big problem. If your problem affects just you and your five friends, it's not going to be a big enough problem to interest investors. Investors are looking for people tackling big problems that potentially affect millions of people. Now, understand me when I say big problems. We don't need to be solving world peace or Einstein-type problems. The problem you are solving simply needs to be a problem that affects many people, ideally millions of people. The issue needs to be a problem that you can see, that is significant to you, and that affects many other people, too. The best businesses start with a simple problem that affects the founder or their family, and they set out to solve their issue. That's the beauty of problem-solving: we solve the problems we can see, which is why women must also be at the table solving problems. Only you will see certain problems, and only you will be able to solve them.

It's not unusual for founders to completely misunderstand the one problem their business solves. I know that sounds counterintuitive, because the wheels are turning and the business is going, but the founders are not necessarily grasping the core of the problem they are addressing with their business solution. They have a business but not much clarity. Raising capital, however, requires you to clearly understand: what problem am I solving, and why does it matter?

When we created our first version of Under Canvas in 2009, the fundamental idea of the business was to create a way for people to experience and enjoy the outdoors without difficulty or discomfort. That core idea was directly connected to my relationship with my husband and our connected history between Montana and Africa. We were building a bridge between ourselves as a married couple with very different likes and preferences, and we were merging our two histories and experiences. We could not only solve our problem by building a bridge for me to enjoy the outdoors with my husband, but could, in turn, also create a bridge for other people. We realized that the bridge between us could be a luxurious tent, and this could potentially be a point of connection for other people like us.

Your Personal Problem

Being personally connected to the problem is the starting point for building something of substance and demonstrates a commitment because you care about solving it. If you are connected to the problem, you'll care about it, understand it, and create a better solution. You will also be infinitely more convincing to investors if solving this problem matters to you.

Building a great pitch deck is all about telling and selling a great story to convince investors to back your vision and help you solve the problem you see. Ask yourself, what is it you care about? What problems or opportunities (the other way of viewing a problem) can you see around you that affect you, your family, or your community? Is there something you can see or can imagine that others can't? Could you make something possible that could make others' lives easier, better, simpler?

It's easy to assume that solving a problem or coming up with a unique idea has to be something huge like discovering relativity or something eternally significant like ending world hunger. This is not so. The problems that need solving simply need to be significant to you because, chances are, if they are significant to you, they are significant to many other people, too. Most successful businesses don't start with a plan to revolutionize the world completely, although they might eventually do that. Much more commonly, the best businesses start with a simple problem that affects the founder or their family, and they set out to solve their own personal issue. What is it that you can see from the perspective of your unique experiences, interests, background, race, gender, and geography?

Take inspiration from some of the following women I am now investing in with our venture capital fund that invests in women entrepreneurs in Africa, who just like you, are taking action to solve the problems they can see.

Ego Iwegbu, a British Nigerian entrepreneur, launched a makeup brand for acne-prone sensitive skin, The Good Mineral (www.thegoodmineral.com). As an acne sufferer herself, she wanted to make cosmetic products that not only covered up blemishes and imperfections, making you look and feel better, but that did not irritate sensitive skin.

Claudia Castellanos, a Colombian Eswatini entrepreneur, wanted to create access for rural, small-scale African female farmers to large commercial markets, getting them a fair price for their produce and creating new routes for export products. She founded Black Mamba (www.blackmambachilli.com), an ethical specialty food company producing foods that are good for you, the planet, and rural communities.

Michele Carelse, a South African Clinical Psychologist, founded Feel Good Health (www.feelgoodhealth.co.za), one of the largest online health retailers in South Africa that now carries over three thousand products. She decided to bring alternative, natural, and herbal medicines mainstream to a broader South African market by creating an online natural health store.

A fellow member of the EY Entrepreneurial Winning Women: Fran Dunaway, from Washington, United States, and a member of the LGBTQ+ (lesbian, gay, bisexual, transgender, queer plus) community, created a gender-neutral underwear company, providing clothing solutions for a community typically not catered to. TomBoyX clothing (www.tomboyx.com) can now be found in Target stores across the US as well as online. Regardless of sexual orientation or gender identification, TomBoyX is a brand that wants to make you feel and look good.

Lori Torres, from California, United States, realized with the rapid increase of online shopping that apartment buildings increasingly had nowhere to store packages while their residents were out at work. She developed smart lockers for her company, Parcel Pending (www.parcelpending.com), to install in apartment buildings, grocery stores, and retailers for customers to have their online purchases securely stored until they can be retrieved.

Nicole Smith, from Victoria, Canada, was frustrated coming back from vacation without great photos of her family. She wanted special moments to be beautifully captured and to explore new places with a local guide who could capture the adventure candidly. She founded Flytographer (www.flytographer.com) to create a network of photographers around the world to ensure that the clients' vacation pictures would be as amazing as their experiences.

All of these women started with a problem that they could see, that affected them, and that they cared about. Their passion and determination to solve their own problem led them to find a solution and build a company to solve the same problem for many other people. None of these women were experts; none of these women had done previously what they do now. Nicole is not a professional photographer. Lori isn't a designer or manufacturer of smart lockers. Fran had never designed clothes before, Michele had never built an online platform, nor had Claudia manufactured chili sauce and sold it around the world. Ego is not a cosmetologist. All of these women, as brilliant as they are, saw a problem and took action. They quieted their doubts and they got to work, believing they should and could build big companies.

Grit

Why do you need to care about your idea? Because building big businesses is hard. If you don't care enough, you won't be able to go the distance. You will give up too easily when the going gets tough. You won't stick it out when things don't go to plan and you won't have a sufficient inner commitment to making your solution a reality. Investors know that building big businesses is grueling and challenging. They understand that the journey takes commitment, tenacity, and the ability to keep getting up after you get knocked down. Determining whether or not the problem matters to you is part of the process of figuring out if you will have what it takes. If your solution matters to you and you can communicate it, you are much more likely to be investable.

To communicate the problem you are solving well, you've got to be able to do so succinctly. Your problem should not be a whole paragraph on a slide; it should be one sentence or one bullet point. Ask yourself, can you say out loud in one sentence the problem your business is addressing? Can you simplify it into an easy-to-understand concept? For Under Canvas, the problem we were solving was the lack of access to the outdoors for those who would never consider camping out in the wilderness. By creating a bridge for Jake and me between each other and the wilderness, we created a bridge for others to access places they would never normally go. This was the heart of our problem—the outdoors is inaccessible to many, many people. We must be able to communicate the problem we are solving and why it matters clearly. If you don't understand the heart of your problem, you'll limit your ability to grow and scale. The entrepreneur who understands the importance of this will discover a doorway to literally changing the world. I realize that "changing the world" is an ambitious idea that has been so carelessly thrown about in pitch meetings that it has become cliché. But, when I imagine that new world, it is composed of each one of us changing our separate places in the world, solving the problems we can see, attaining fulfillment, satisfaction, well-being, and financial freedom, and in doing so, revolutionizing our planet, and making our individual and collective worlds a better place.

It's Time

The heart of the problem for women entrepreneurs is that very often, we need to think bigger. More women need to make big things happen if we're going to move our world forward, creating a more equitable world for all. We must put aside our doubts, develop new mantras in our heads, ignore our lack of confidence and our nagging insecurities, and remember the female pioneers who have gone before us and whose shoulders we can stand upon. We quite simply do not have the time or luxury to allow our own insecurities or outdated beliefs to slow us down, to tell us what we can or cannot do, and to keep us in a box. The world needs us to think big, be brave, and take on big challenges. We only need to take on one problem we can see and offer a creative solution for it. We need to start where we are, with a problem we care about and are connected to. Then, we get to work to craft our solution and build our products and services, putting one foot in front of the other, taking one step at a time. When we launched Under Canvas, we knew we wanted to be a bridge and create access to the outdoors—that was the problem we wanted to solve. How exactly we were going to do that, we weren't 100 percent sure. Before we arrived at our final scalable business model, we had several false starts and failed attempts to create a viable, successful business. Rome is never built in a day—but understanding the problem you want to solve is where you start. That's where your pitch deck starts and the concept for your business idea begins to address the heart of the problem.

Questions for Reflection

- What role has grit played in your journey thus far? Have you had to pick yourself up after a seismic failure and reimagine a way forward?
- How big are you currently thinking? Now multiply that by one hundred.

- What do you think it would take to help you make something big happen?
- How does impostor syndrome affect you? What does your inner voice whisper to you?
- What is the heart of the problem you are trying to solve? Can you communicate that problem in one sentence?
- Why do you care about that problem? How are you connected to the problem you can see? Does this problem affect millions of other people?

Slide Two of the Pitch Deck: The Problem

Write in one sentence the problem your business is solving in a punchy, clear, gripping way. Note that it is so much easier to describe your solution than your problem, but don't be tempted to give your solution away just yet. Imagine you are on the American classic TV show Jeopardy and that you can only communicate the question to your solution. Tell us the big problem you can see and show us that you care about it.

2

Solutions Require Failure

Those who dare to fail miserably can achieve greatly.

—John F. Kennedy

In 2009, amid the continuing Global Economic Crisis, we launched our fledging recreation of the African safari experience on the Great Plains of Montana at Jake's family's farm. We started with four beautiful safari tents and a small lodge building that overlooked a vast, impressive prairie that seemed to go on forever. Jake designed and built our camp with the help of some willing friends and after six months of laboring, we were ready to open our doors to the public. Our first official guests ended up being a TV film crew who wanted to showcase the opening of our new property. We were excited. Jake would offer guided tours of the property and I would become the chief cook and bottle washer.

We had created a picture-perfect setting, but the business was a disaster. It turned out that hardly anyone wanted to go to the middle of nowhere in Montana to stay in a fancy tent, despite how fantastic my cooking was! We quickly realized we were going to seriously struggle to earn a living from what we had created and were faced with the compounding financial challenge of failure after failure. The daunting possibility of complete and utter financial ruin was emotionally distressing, to say the least. But we were determined that this wasn't going to be the end of the story. While no one wanted to come to northern rural Montana, we constantly fielded phone calls from people asking where they could purchase our beautiful tents. People wanted to use them for weddings, large events, and family gatherings all over the country. So, when the phone rang, instead of being disappointed or frustrated that the caller didn't want to stay with us, we offered to bring our tents to their event. The market was telling us they wanted our tents. They just didn't want them where we had set them up. This new development was our opportunity to pivot and create our second iteration as a tented events company. Our ability to learn and adapt quickly became one of our greatest assets. Instead of accepting failure, we realized that we didn't yet have the right solution for the problem we wanted to solve.

As we traveled across the United States, taking our tents to people for weddings, family reunions, and festivals, we came upon our second realization: we didn't just have a unique product; we were providing a lifestyle experience. We realized that we were creating a bridge that enabled people to not only enjoy the outdoors in a comfortable, easy way but that we were also able to help people connect as they unplugged from their busy technological lives. We could help bridge not only the cavern between people and the outdoors but also the cavern that twenty-first century daily life creates between people. Now, we were providing extraordinary, memory-making recreational experiences all over the country. Our customers could disconnect from the pressures of their lives and reconnect with the people they love, all while making amazing memories with their friends and family. This realization sparked our next iteration.

We asked ourselves, "Instead of waiting for the phone to ring with questions about where to purchase or rent our tents, could we take our tents to the locations where large groups of people are already going and erect a tented hotel type of experience for people to check into for several nights?" In other words, could we proactively do something to create our own future rather than wait for business to come to us? Jim Collins, author of *Great by Choice*, defines this characteristic of being proactive and making your own luck as one of the determining factors of companies that go on to grow exponentially, often growing to ten times their size in relatively short order.[1] He realized that leaders and founders who are proactive about harnessing their own luck and even turning bad luck into good luck are infinitely more likely to go on to build big businesses. For us, thinking proactively enabled us to give birth to Under Canvas, the business model we ultimately built into a valuable company worth over $100 million.

It is easy to look at businesses we deem successful and assume they were an instant success. Rarely is this the case. The huge conglomerates of our day, Google, Apple, Facebook, and Amazon, were all also once scrappy start-ups, trying to figure out a plan to acquire users and develop exponentially scalable business models. For example, Facebook had numerous iterations before it ultimately became Facebook as we know it today. It was launched in 2003 as FaceMash, an online service developed for Harvard students to judge the attractiveness of their fellow students. Thankfully, it quickly transformed into The Facebook, a broader college networking tool, before finally becoming the more recognizable platform we know today, the largest online social networking site on the planet.

Successful solutions to stubborn problems often require an enormous amount of iteration and failure, because discovering what doesn't work often helps us to realize what does.

We didn't build our valuable business overnight. It took us three years to go from our initial embryonic idea of a small Montana-based glamping experience to a tent rental company to the idea of creating luxury-tented hotel experiences in existing vacation locations. Three years to develop a business model with the potential for significant growth and scalability, a model that not only allows us to earn a living but also create significant value and impact.

We might have reached our successful business model sooner if we had realized that one of the keys to building a big, successful business is accepting that the precursor to success is a significant amount of reiteration and failure. Realizing what isn't working or isn't scalable and understanding what the market is telling you is critical to adjusting your business solution to transform it into a viable, scalable business and finding what business analysts identify as product-market fit.

Product-Market Fit

Product-market fit simply means that your business offers a solution that works and for which there is demand, as demonstrated by people being willing to pay for it. It means there is alignment between the company's product offering and the needs and desires of its target market audience, resulting in strong sales and customer satisfaction. When we've got product-market fit, we should be able to see that a product or service is selling well or gaining users quickly because it meets the needs of the market. Having a great solution is proved by customers wanting your solution and using your product or services in increasing measures.

Tech companies often don't measure sales or revenue in their early days because frequently, tech will be given away for free. Typically, they will be measuring users instead. Showing rapid growth of users would similarly demonstrate having found product-market fit. Investors want to see that people want the amazing products or services that you are offering. Therefore, finding the perfect fit with your customer base determines whether you've got a great solution to the problem you are trying to solve.

How, then, do we discover if we've got product-market fit? What are the keys that will help us arrive at this elusive destination?

Fail Fast

One of the most valuable pieces of advice for entrepreneurs I've heard in recent times hails from Uri Levine, founder and co-creator of Waze and Moovit and a two-time unicorn (a start-up that is valued at $1 billion or more). Uri is a staunch proponent of the need to fail fast. He argues that to discover a successful business solution and to find product-market fit, we must fail as fast as we possibly can in order to eliminate ideas that don't work so we can discover the idea that does.[2] Entrepreneurs should think like scientists, accepting there will be many proposed solutions that will not work or only partially work. We must recognize that our job is to eliminate those non-viable solutions as fast as possible so we can discover the idea that works.

On a practical level, what does homing in on viable solutions look like? Just like when developing a new drug or vaccine or making a scientific breakthrough, we must vigorously test our hypothesis, making tweaks and adjustments until we discover the solution that works. Levine, similarly, argues for an aggressive approach to revising the product to fit its purpose and customer needs better, adjusting and reiterating over and over and over until the customer indicates we are on to something.[3] Success requires that we test, test, and keep testing our ideas. We must not get stuck on one idea but be prepared to revise, change, adapt, adjust, and reiterate.

It is easier to approach the idea of reiteration when things aren't working and we've got nothing but failure on our hands. Complete failure often forces us to start over or give up. But this idea may be paradoxical to many of us who have created a business experiencing some degree of success. In my own business, for example, we pivoted to an idea that led us to rent our tents for events. That idea enabled us to earn a living and even generate some profit. But this is where "good" is the enemy of "great." We had still not landed on a business model that was scalable or through which we could drive significant growth, even though our event business model was ultimately able to do over seven figures in revenue. Staying with the tented event business model would ensure we stayed in the "small business" category, even though we were able to generate significant revenue.

Our event tent business model was difficult to grow as our solution relied on our customers deciding to have their own glamping event. We could provide inspiration for sure, sharing amazing images of our beautiful tents on social media. Yet despite our best efforts and a considerable amount of energy and money spent on marketing, there was truly little we could do to scale our event business. We hadn't landed on a scalable solution, which is one of the key criteria for being investable. Our lack of scalability meant that we needed to leave behind a good solution (not a complete failure) and continue to iterate it until we found the solution that would be our home run. If we had settled for $1 million in revenue, we would have never built a business that was investable and ultimately exceptionally valuable. This idea of letting go of something good to take hold of something even better is a challenging approach for many women. Being afraid to lose what we've got, what we've worked so hard to achieve, can be a mindset that keeps us thinking and playing small. If we are going to build big businesses, we must learn not to settle for a small game and keep dreaming bigger while continuing to test our ideas on our customers until we land on a scalable idea that has product-market fit.

Product-Market Fit Isn't Perfection

Reaching the point of product-market fit does not mean we need to have a perfect product. You only need to show that you have a scalable idea—a solution that people have shown they want. It does not need to look like a perfectly finished final version, as demonstrated by the first iteration of our tented hotel idea.

In 2012, three years after we originally launched our Montana business, Under Canvas was born when we set up a tented hotel-like experience near Yellowstone National Park. Thousands of people paid to stay with us that first summer season, and this confirmed to Jake and I that we had a market for our ideas beyond our friends and us. We had product-market fit. But the product was far from perfect. The first iteration of Under Canvas wasn't Under Canvas 5.0, which is what exists today—a professional, polished product with great operating systems.

In 2012, we erected thirty-five tents near Yellowstone National Park. Jake and I, our two small children who were nine months and three years old, and an au pair lived in a small, two-bedroom camper on the site. We had five additional employees who helped manage water and sewerage, maintenance, housekeeping, and the front desk.

Almost every day that summer, a rainstorm would come through our camp. One day, at about 5:00 p.m., a huge thunderstorm rolled through the camp with whooshing winds ravaging everything in their path. We evacuated the tents, which was the protocol we had developed on the fly for those scenarios. We announced to our residential customers, "A big storm is coming through; go sit in your car until it passes. It will be fine, but don't sit in the tent." On this occasion, my husband was away at the time, and so I sheltered alone with my two children in our camper.

An avalanche of water fell from the sky. A sharp, loud crack of thunder rumbled across our path as lightning lit up the dark sky, and a rush of shrieking wind rocked our camper so violently that it occurred to me that it could topple over. I considered whether to wrestle with my two children under my arms to get to a car or to stay put. The decision felt impossible. But I had to make one. I stayed in the camper. The wind roared, rocking the camper like a rocking chair for an hour that seemed like an eternity.

Finally, the wind calmed, the rain stopped, and our maintenance person knocked on the door asking, "Are you OK?"

"I'm not OK, I'm not OK," I said between frantic sobs.

Once out of the camper, we surveyed the camp, and almost all of it had been flattened to the ground by the storm. Many of the poles that kept the tents upright were broken, and tents were sprawled all over the ground. The decimation from the storm resembled a disaster area after a hurricane had rolled through. I remember walking through the camp and thinking, "We're done; it's over, there's no coming back from this, and no one will ever pay us again to sleep in our tents because they can't even hold up to the wind."

I cried so hard that my concerned three-year-old asked, "What's the matter, Mummy?" I called my husband, Jake, and said, "We're finished; it's over. There is no coming back from this." In the middle of that overwhelming and devastating moment, my maintenance person said, "Let me speak to him." He took the phone from me and said, "It's not that bad. I think we can put the camp back together." And with that, he rallied our staff, called neighbors in to help us, and our guests returned to help restore the camp to some sense of order. By about 11:00 p.m., we had all the tents back up and everybody back in their beds with clean, dry bedding. Miraculously, not one customer requested a refund.

I wanted an excuse to quit, an excuse to say, "this doesn't work, this can't work, this is too hard, too many things can go wrong, it's too much." I was completely exhausted. We had next to no money. We had started our Montana business with a few thousand dollars from my husband's family, and by this point, three years into our business journey, there was nothing left of that investment. We had no reserves or safety nets other than loving families who would have welcomed us back to their homes to live with them if needed. I do recognize that this was a safety net not everyone has. We were living on food stamps, in a camper with two small children, and had a lot of credit card bills. We financed our third (and final in my mind) reiteration of the business with credit cards, and I constantly struggled to make enough money to pay one credit card after another. I was under constant and extreme stress. Financial stress is one of the biggest drivers of failure and, consequently, the most significant reason many entrepreneurs give up pursuing their solutions. It is quite easy to accept that there simply isn't enough money to carry on.

That night, I wanted an excuse to give up. I didn't get one. Hearing my maintenance person say, "It's not that bad," and seeing the response of our staff, neighbors, and guests pushed me to press forward.

The reality is that we can always come back from something terrible. Every time something doesn't work our way, every time we get knocked down by a disaster like a product flop or no sales, we must remember that we have power over our response to failure. How we respond to both good and bad situations largely determines whether we will succeed or not. We get to choose how we respond and how resilient and smart we will be in response to the situation. Will we allow ourselves to be defined or limited by one failure or even successive failures? Even with financial limitations, the key to not losing momentum is to ask yourself, how creatively can I think about how to make the world's financial systems work for my business? While there may be an absence of money in your bank account, there's no shortage of capital in the world. The question simply becomes how hard you will work and how creative you are willing to be to make something happen. Will you allow failure to not only form you but inform you, teach you, and reveal a new path ahead? We do not need to be afraid of failure or of things not going the way we had planned, as every disaster creates an opportunity for success if we harness it correctly. Being willing to fail, experiment, and put out imperfection into the world is our road map to building something great. We need to realize that we don't have to do everything perfectly the first time to succeed. Our imperfections and original iterations, as disastrous as they might be at first, will often be the first steps on the path of building something big.

Failure is Learning

For many of us women, having successful careers has required being flawless and perfect, not putting a step wrong, and being better than everyone else to be accepted into male-dominated workplaces. Women are often afraid to fail. Yet, to succeed in entrepreneurship, we must re-condition our minds to embrace the concept of failure. How do we now wrap our arms around the concept of failure as not only a requirement for innovation but the pathway guiding our journey toward success?

We must shake off our absolute perspectives on failure: "If I fail, then I'm a failure." Instead of believing our failures somehow define and reduce us or call into question our credibility, we must simply see all failures, big and small, as learning, lessons we acquired the hard and often expensive way. The failures and mistakes I have made in business have cost me more than an expensive education at Harvard or Princeton, but we must accept that when we pioneer new ground or step into new arenas, we are not going to know everything we need to know even if we did have an expensive education. We will still not have acquired all the knowledge or skills we need to succeed. Scientists do not know all the components of a new drug without first conducting experiments. Neither will you hit a home run without failing over and over. Failure is your way of testing the waters; failure allows you to make mistakes, to get it wrong, for things to go wrong, and not be perfect. Every failure, however, enables us to learn things we may never have realized otherwise. It is the key ingredient in allowing us to learn what elements will create success. It is our failures that allow us to fix the glitches in our operations and remodel or revamp our products to better suit their purpose. We can use the knowledge we gain from our failures to build upon our realizations and move us closer to creating the perfect solution.

If we embrace failure as a learning opportunity and shake off the shadow and shame it casts over us, we will be infinitely more likely to solve problems, create solutions that change other people's lives for the better, and move our world forward. The key is to get used to the feeling of failure and move forward anyway.

Failure and Fear

In her book *Big Magic*, Elizabeth Gilbert tells a story of her struggles dealing with fear.[4] She recounts the paralysis she felt any time she had a great idea for a book. She would find herself stopped in her tracks, firmly stuck, unable to write a single word. Until one day, she realized fear wasn't going to leave her alone. Fear was going to be a companion with whom she would need to learn to share her life. When she realized that her fear was her new daily companion, she realized that she had a choice. She could choose to listen to fear and stay stuck, or she could recognize the voice of fear and carry on anyway. Gilbert shares a picture of fear she crafted in her imagination, who wanted to take the driving seat in her life and dictate where she went and what she did. While fear might have to travel with her on the journey, it didn't need to be in the driver's seat. From that day on, Gilbert allowed her fear to come along on her creative writing adventures but designated that fear would need to sit in the backseat of the car, not touch the radio, and not give her instructions from the back. Gilbert is teaching us that we can learn to live with fear, embrace its presence, and carry on anyway.

No one likes feeling afraid. No one likes failing. It's not a matter of saying, "Great, I failed; bring it on!" Instead, it is a grueling and painful experience that really hurts. Failure for entrepreneurs frequently means hearing "no" repeatedly, experiencing constant rejection, having too few sales, not getting your product in front of enough customers, or not getting the results you want. Failure drains our emotional reserves and causes us to question everything. However, if we don't learn from our failures, then the only alternative is to give up. We can either surrender our dream or press forward. The key is to stay the course, reiterating as we grow and finding a solution by learning and continuously trying something new, testing everything until, eventually, we reach a breakthrough. Breakthroughs are always hard-won. Very often, the difference between those who succeed at bringing their solutions to life and those who do not is simply longevity—staying in the game long enough to get a breakthrough. If we had not persevered through those first early years in Montana when financial resources were at their lowest and if we had not continued to pivot and adapt our business model, enduring endless disasters, we would have never got to the point where we had a business model that could be something great. Endure and lever failure until it yields success.

Harnessing No

Anouck Gotlib, chief executive officer (CEO) and cofounder of Belgian Boys, a breakfast and sweet treats company, wanted to bring stroopwafels, French crepes, and the delicious foods of her childhood in Belgium to the United States. Anouck dreamed of introducing America to the sweet treats she loved and missed by creating products that could revolutionize the breakfast table in the United States. For years, she met with retail store buyers who didn't understand her vision to merchandise refrigerated breakfast staples as opposed to frozen as they had always been sold in US retailers. From 2015 all the way through 2019, she pitched her idea to sell her crepes, pancakes, and waffles in the refrigeration section of the grocery store, right alongside the milk, yogurt, eggs, and orange juice people pick up for breakfast. She wanted her products to be sold as fresh breakfast items that Americans could eat every single day. She believed she could make her category of breakfast foods mainstream. However, she was faced with a barrage of rejections, with buyer after buyer telling her, "No, those products are frozen products and should only go in the frozen section." For years, she followed the buyer's advice and merchandised the brand in the frozen section alongside American legacy brands, but she knew that she could appeal better to the mainstream consumer in the refrigerated section. Breakfast, unlike any other meal of the day, is a meal that we often consume on the run, and we often eat the same thing repeatedly. She wanted to be the go-to brand of choice for delicious, refrigerated breakfast foods that would be quick and easy to prepare if they didn't come frozen. Time after time, buyers consistently told her, "No, you are frozen breakfast; that's the category." She realized she was trying to create a category that did not exist yet but was determined to keep presenting her idea until, finally, someone took her seriously. She believed if she could just test her hypothesis, she could either put the idea behind her, or she would be proven right.

Finally, in 2019, Walmart agreed to try her idea. They agreed to pilot Belgian Boys products in the refrigeration section in sixty-five stores, and as Anouck had suspected all along, her products did exceptionally well. They performed five times better than when hidden away in frozen foods. Walmart rolled out the concept the following year to three hundred stores in total, and in 2021, Target also said they would experiment with the concept. After four years of consistent rejections, she finally got an elusive *yes*, which triggered another yes, which in turn started a barrage of yeses. The data she gathered from those initial retailers regarding the performance of her products as refrigerated breakfast items confirmed the reality that Belgian Boys waffles, pancakes, and crepes could indeed be everyday breakfast items, consumed daily and purchased weekly. The volume of sales she could make for both her own brand and the retailers drastically increased. In 2022, Belgian Boys products were in over seven thousand stores across the United States in nearly all the main grocery brands, putting her well on her way to becoming a well-known, mainstream brand.

Every *no* was exceptionally painful to hear. Every no felt like a personal rejection, causing her to doubt and question herself and feel like she was just not good enough. Yet upon reflection, she realized critically that every no was simply a "not yet," "not right now," and "not for me," which, of course, is different from "not ever," "not you," or "you suck!" While a no might feel personal, it is not. Women cannot afford the luxury of getting stuck because of someone else's rejection. When Anouck started to hear the noes as "not yet" and "not for me," she started to ask herself, "OK, if not you, then who?" or "What do I need to do on my end for that no to become a yes?" She knew she had to test her hypothesis. She didn't want to give up until she'd at least tested her idea, and that meant convincing at least one buyer to try out her idea and potentially take her products mainstream. She adjusted her approach and started to think about how she could add value to the retailer. She started presenting them with an opportunity to do something new, to drive sales they would not drive otherwise, creating incremental value. She realized if she was ever going to convince anyone that her idea would be successful, she needed to reposition her pitch and demonstrate how she could add value to the store's bottom line. By creating a new category, retailers would not be asking consumers to choose between one brand and another but to purchase additional items they wouldn't normally have purchased. Rethinking her approach, turned those noes into big yeses, creating a win not only for her own company but for the retailers and consumers, too.

Anouck persevered to get her breakthrough because she had big dreams. She didn't want to settle for being an occasional buy. She wanted to increase the volume of her sales and make European foods mainstream. If she hadn't persisted with getting her products into the refrigeration section, she would have limited her company's potential for scale and growth. She had to persevere long enough and keep getting back up after hearing no to get her big breakthrough.

This level of persistence requires enormous grit and a willingness to face repeated failures to stay in the game. Women need to dig deep, develop the mental attitude required to test their ideas over and over, and learn from every iteration. Anouck realized her approach to retailers wasn't working, and so she adjusted her pitch. We must recognize when something isn't working and change track quickly to not waste time and money. Similarly, holding on too long to an average solution or idea can be just as devastating as giving up too quickly. If I had kept version 1.0 of Under Canvas, I would have never built a valuable business. If Anouck had stayed in frozen produce, her company would not be experiencing hypergrowth. The key to the evolution of your solution is to realize that sometimes you must sacrifice the thing that keeps the lights on to be able to create a big, wildly successful company. We must be prepared to take big risks and not play it safe if we are going to make big things happen.

If your idea barely works, just about works, or is average, it's time to reiterate and pivot. Do not settle; instead, take the time to learn from the valuable information the market is telling you, adjust your products or your approach, reiterate over and over and over again, and most importantly, do not give up until you get the breakthrough you believe is possible.

Bringing a successful solution to the market is not easy or quick. It took us three years to arrive at the starting line with a business model that was scalable and had growth potential. Arriving at that point was only the beginning of the journey. Many more reiterations and adjustments were still to come. The path between origination and big success will require a considerable amount of failure, but know that every test, every no, and every moment of disaster moves you closer to success, closer to a yes, closer to your dream. This can only happen, however, if you make fear sit in the backseat, don't take failure personally, and instead learn, adapt, adjust, and listen to what the market wants to tell you.

Our Solutions

Anouck's business is solving the problem of the lack of availability in the US of the sweet European foods of her youth. Her solution is to bring fresh European food to your breakfast table every morning. My solution was to create beautiful, tented hotels across the US to enable people to access the outdoors and connect with nature and each other. What is the solution that you are uniquely bringing to the world? Maybe your solution has been done before, but you are bringing it in a new way in a new place. Maybe you are creating a new category or new industry. Maybe you are solving something for a specific group of people whose needs haven't been addressed. Maybe you are creating technology to do something faster, better, or more easily than we can today. In your pitch deck, tell us about your solution to the specific problem you are aiming to solve. Demonstrate that you've tested your idea and that your consumer wants your solution.

Remember, whatever the magnitude of the problem you are trying to address, the world needs you to bring your solution in the unique way that only you can. The world needs you to persevere long enough, to embrace the failures and lessons along the way to create products and services that we all need and want.

Demonstrating that you've found product-market fit and not settling for mediocre sales or growth will go a long way to pique investors' interest in your business. Don't be afraid to fail. Embrace failure as your trusted friend on a vigorous journey toward your dreams.

I meet entrepreneurs in various parts of Africa every day who are figuring out solutions to some of the world's biggest, most pressing problems and who have infinitely fewer resources and a lot more to contend with than the average person in Western, developed nations. South Africa today is experiencing significant power outages, causing the electricity to be off for up to six to eight hours a day. But meet Chilufya Mutale, who is building a Challenger Bank for the 500 million people in Africa who do not have access to banking services or capital and are considered unbanked or un-bankable. Or Lauren Anderson, who is revolutionizing access to quality education for Africa's students. Or Meg Faure, who is reinventing preschool education advocating for the importance of play in nurturing Africa's infants in their first thousand days of life.

We can build successful big businesses; but we must develop our inner strength to cope with the inevitable blows, difficulties, and failures that are a significant part of the entrepreneurial journey. As female entrepreneurs, we must not only expect failure but be willing to harness and learn from it.

Questions for Reflection

- Are you settling for a business that's smaller than it could be? Is there something you are afraid to let go of to take hold of something better?
- Do you need to make friends with the idea that you will need to fail often and significantly to arrive at your desired destination? What needs to shift in your mind regarding failure?
- Are you currently testing your ideas rigorously? If not, why not? What else could you be doing to test, test, test?
- What have you learned so far from what has and has not worked? Where do you need to adapt?
- Have you found product-market fit yet? Do you have a business model that could scale exponentially?
- What is your business solution in one sentence?

Slide Three of the Pitch Deck: The Solution

Tell us in as few words as possible your solution to the problem you've outlined on slide two. You'll get a chance to describe your product or service in detail on the next slide. This page is your opportunity to show us what solution you've discovered and to indicate you've found product-market fit.

3

The Product Is Also You

*If you want something you've never had, you must be
willing to do something you've never done.*

—Thomas Jefferson*

One cold, wintery evening toward the end of 2010, our phone rang. It was a
familiar but unusual call. "We love your tents; where can we get them from?"
The call was from a British event producer who was planning to host a new music
festival in Long Island, New York, the following year. "We're looking for one
hundred and fifty tents for our music festival next summer. We want to create a
glamping camp for our festivalgoers. Could you tell us where we could get your
tents from?" Jake had personally designed our tents, and they were beautiful but
not originally intended to be set up temporarily for an event. Even though Jake's
designs weren't designed specifically for event use and we didn't have one hundred and fifty tents, he had the courage and confidence to say they could get them
directly from us! We had no idea how we were going to pull this off, but he said
we'd help anyway, somehow sensing this was a big moment for us.

We had weathered two seasons of our four-tent camp in rural Montana, and
we were struggling to make ends meet. Jake was working as a contractor through
the winter during our off-season to try and keep us afloat financially, but we had
no idea how we were going to afford to manufacture hundreds of tents for a festival in just seven months. It seemed crazy, especially after the event producer

---

*This quote is likely falsely attributed to Thomas Jefferson.

called us again a couple of months later to say they would rather not buy the tents and would rather rent them instead. We had encouraged them to pay us a deposit for the tents so we could place an order for newly designed tents suitable for events with the manufacturers. But now they were saying they didn't want to purchase the tents. Our hearts were racing. We had taken a significant risk by placing a huge order for hundreds of tents, leaving us financially vulnerable to the upfront cost of the tents. This potential client explained that they needed someone to manage the setup and takedown of the tents and be responsible for the glamping village. They asked if they could rent the tents from us instead of purchasing them so that they didn't have to worry about the tents before or after the event. We looked at each other and asked, "What are the precise dates of the event?" I was pregnant with our second child at the time, and the festival was just one week before my due date. But we knew that we had to say yes! We told the event producer that the rental price of the tents would be the same as buying them, except that we would include the setup and takedown in the original price. They miraculously agreed. We had no idea how we were going to pull this off; we had no crew, no experience setting up hundreds of tents, and no idea how we were going to transport everything we would need across the country from Montana to New York and navigate having a baby all at the same time. But we knew we had to take the risk. Despite having a complicated delivery with my first child, this moment felt too big to turn down.

Within just a few months from that call, we rallied three friends to come to join Jake for a fun weekend in New York and hoped we could hire more laborers in New York to help set up the tents. The guys had just three days to set up and furnish all one hundred and fifty tents. They worked around the clock, night and day, attempting to get everything ready in time. Jake's three friends ended up being the only capable laborers we had. The weather also did not fully cooperate, and with humidity and temperatures well over 90°F, the task was monumental. With just hours to spare, the guys hammered their last tent peg and stood back in awe at what they'd created. Since the festival only lasted three days, they had only a brief chance to catch their breath before it was time to take it all down again post-event. Knowing that I was due to give birth any day, Jake organized the guys to complete the pack up of all the tents into storage pods without him, and he left to fly back to the family. I went into labor within hours of his arrival home, and our second son was born healthy and strong just a few hours after that. He made it. We made it.

That event was a huge catalyst in our lives. Not only did it propel us into the tented event business, but it also gave us an enormous resource—tents. If we had sold those tents, we would have made a small amount of profit from that one event. But by renting those tents, while we made no money from the event after all our costs to transport, set up, take down, and store the tents, we ended up with an incredible asset that we could harness to build the second and third iterations of our business. It was worth it to take the enormous risk, going all in. You can never be sure if the sacrifices and commitments you make will pay off, but it's people who take big risks and who demonstrate enormous tenacity who ultimately will attract others to believe and invest in them.

Investing in People

Who is more important in a horse race? The jockey or the horse? Of course, both are essential; a jockey couldn't win a race without a horse, or a horse without a jockey. Yet 99.9 percent of investors would say that when they invest in a company, they are making a bet on the jockey or the founder. Investors know that regardless of how brilliant or outstanding a business idea is (and they do want great solutions to clear problems), ultimately, it is people that make things happen. A great idea can only become an outstanding business if the founder executes their vision and brings their idea to life. An average idea has a much better chance of becoming extraordinary in the hands of an outstanding person, compared with a brilliant idea in the hands of an average person. Investors invest in people first and foremost.

In the excitement of presenting your products and services, which are what you get to showcase on the fourth page of your deck, it is easy to forget that investors are not only looking for great ideas but also for great people with the ability, tenacity, and determination to make big things happen. Your product could be the most brilliant idea anyone has ever heard of, but if you don't also demonstrate your ability to execute it, you will not get an investment. How do we, therefore, highlight not only our products and services but also ourselves?

This fourth slide in the pitch deck (The Product) showcases your product or service—how it works, what it does, and what it looks like. It also showcases you because your product is an expression of you, what you think is possible, and what you can pull off. When you pitch your business idea for investment, you are also selling yourself.

Let's explore three distinct characteristics that indicate to investors that you might have what it takes to build something big.

All In

In 2013, when Lori Torres came up with the idea for her company, Parcel Pending, a smart locker company for apartment buildings and retailers, she knew in her bones that she was on to something. Only one other time in her life did she recall having this feeling, and that was thirty-two years earlier, when she had the idea for Elf on the Shelf. She didn't pursue that idea, and of course, Elf on the Shelf went on to become one of the biggest family Christmas traditions around the Western world. She had missed out on making something big happen once before, and so with this new idea, she was determined to make it happen. Yet she faced the insurmountable challenge of being the breadwinner in her family. She had a successful career in real estate, working for one of the largest and most prestigious firms in the country, and her family relied on her to earn a living. How could she possibly even think about giving up her income to start a business? Could she ask her family to sacrifice their comfortable lives to pursue what was no more than a hunch? The idea just wouldn't leave her alone, and she knew she had to take a chance and make a big bet to try and get Parcel Pending off the ground. She not only gave up her well-paying job, but she also sold the dream home the family was living in. A home that had every amenity you could imagine, a place where her kids had thrown amazing birthday parties and they had made so many great memories together. Yet all of that was still not enough to pay off outstanding debts and give her the runway she needed to create Parcel Pending's first smart lockers. So, she also went to her mother, who had never made more income than forty thousand dollars a year, and asked if she would take a loan out against her home. Not only did she sell her own home, but she also asked her mom if she would put her home at risk too. She went all in on her hunch that Parcel Pending would not only be a success but that smart lockers would eventually be in every apartment building in the United States and the company would ultimately be sold for one hundred million dollars.

Within one year of quitting her job and selling her home, Lori had created her minimum viable product—her first smart lockers to go into apartment buildings. Her lockers would help solve the package crisis for property management companies by creating a safe place for residents' online orders to go once they arrived at their destination. Apartment buildings would be able to install smart lockers for each resident and safely place their packages within their locker. She didn't know it then, but by the end of 2014, with her first order for lockers already secured and investors interested to help her continue to grow, she had also secured her family's future. Within just six short years of her original all-in moment, Parcel Pending would be sold for one hundred million dollars, and her mother's home loan would turn into a one-million-dollar return.

Very often, turning your vision and idea into a successful business depends on your ability to go all in and commit to its fulfillment. When you are all in and everything depends on you making your business work, your level of determination will be exponentially greater than if you are halfhearted about your idea. If the business hasn't cost you something, such as your comfort, security, or bank balance, the likelihood of getting to your breakthrough moment will be greatly diminished. Not only will it be easier to give up, but it will also be more unlikely that investors will believe in what you're doing or take you seriously.

Investors assess founders, rightly or wrongly, on what it has already cost the founder to get to this point in time. Does the founder have a mindset that's able to embrace taking big risks? Having your blood, sweat, skin, and tears in the game will be a critical sight for investors. Venture capitalists look for people who are prepared to go all in on making their dreams a reality, hungry people, people with drive, and people who recognize that achieving success requires sacrifice.

Making Sacrifices Today

In the 1960s, a Stanford professor named Walter Mischel began conducting a series of psychological studies.[1] He tested hundreds of children around the ages of four and five and revealed what he believed to be one of the most important characteristics for success in health, work, and life. In his experiment, children were offered one marshmallow to be eaten now or two marshmallows if they were willing to wait fifteen minutes for the researcher to return to the room. If they couldn't wait and ate the marshmallow right away, the researcher would not reward them with a second marshmallow. Over a period of forty years, following those same children who participated in that test, the researchers discovered that the children who could wait for two marshmallows seemed to succeed in life in whatever capacity they were measuring. He discovered that our ability to delay our gratification and sacrifice something in the immediate for the possibility of something more in the future was a key indicator of how outwardly successful (in generic terms) people would be. The two-marshmallow group tended to have higher SAT scores, better responses to stress, better social skills, and generally do better in life overall.

People who can build valuable businesses are two-marshmallow people. They know it's necessary to make sacrifices today to make something better happen tomorrow. In a technological world where waiting for anything feels nonsensical, being reminded that building or creating anything of lasting significance or scale takes time and sacrifice is a hard pill to swallow. As unpopular as it is to hear, success requires sacrifice, effort, and pain.

Our first year opening our first tented hotel in Yellowstone was brutal and intense in every way you can imagine—from extreme weather to lack of privacy to sixteen-hour workdays. We reached a pivotal moment. We were three years into the business—three years of living on a financial knife edge—but we hoped we were on the precipice of a breakthrough. We had to decide whether we were either all in and would do everything we could to make the business work, or if we were done and ready to give up.

As I mentioned, I so desperately wanted to give up because our day-to-day was so unbearably hard and stressful, but we realized this was our last shot. We thought, "If this doesn't work, we've got nothing left." We didn't want to live with any regrets, knowing we hadn't given our ideas our all and could potentially miss out on what could have been. So, we gave it everything we had, committing to discomfort on every level. We went all in, not knowing if our sacrifices would pay off. That's always the risk. Our all-in moments may or may not yield the outcome we desire. Yet without going all in, we almost always ensure the outcomes we want remain out of reach.

If you know you have a great solution, double down and bet on yourself. Show the world how serious you are. You must take yourself seriously before you can expect anyone else to do the same. Investors are going to be looking at what truly matters to you and what you are prepared to do to bring your vision to life.

Do you have what it takes to go the distance to make something big happen? What sacrifices have you made to bring your business idea to life? Did you need to sell a car to get yourself started? Maybe you remortgaged or even sold your home. Did you or your partner give up your job to start work on this project? Did you sacrifice all your spare time, working late into the night, to get your side hustle off the ground? How are you demonstrating that you are all in on your idea? Are you prepared to wait for a second marshmallow and make sacrifices today?

Taking Big Risks

In addition to making sacrifices, taking risks is also going to be a recurring part of your life if you want to build something big. Risk exposes us to the possibility of loss or harm, yet it is a necessary part of the journey to achieve a big goal or gain a reward. Making decisions or taking actions that have an uncertain outcome and the potential for negative consequences is a constant part of the roller coaster of entrepreneurship, and it doesn't get easier over time either. Every time we are faced with a decision that could cost us significantly if we get it wrong, it is a difficult decision to take the risk. Yet author Rob Bell insists that "risk is where the life is."[2] When we take risks, we are fully alive, pursuing our dreams, and taking bold steps to make things happen. Entrepreneurs who shy away from big, bold, risky moves, don't take chances, or don't go out on a limb are likely to get stuck very quickly and are unlikely to see the realization of big rewards.

When we first decided to see if we could try and create a tented hotel outside of Yellowstone National Park, we took on multiple new risks. We had to lease land, which would require us to commit to paying a monthly land fee. Even though we had acquired tents through the large event in New York, we had to buy several hundred thousand dollars' worth of equipment, furniture, and bedding. We had to design and build bathroom units to be ready to use by our advertised opening date. And all without knowing if anyone would want to stay in a tented hotel. We had no experience running a hotel before, let alone a tented one. We had no certainty that our idea was a good one. It was an enormous financial risk to us, a risk that almost certainly would have forced us into bankruptcy if we were not able to pull it off. Yet the possibility of making something extraordinary happen was also there. There was the possibility that we could create something magical, that we could build a scalable business that would transform not only our own lives but many others as well. It was a risk that required us to inhale a big, deep breath and take the leap. We took the plunge, not knowing if we would find a place to land on the other side or if we would come crashing down to earth with a thud. Taking a chance and making a leap is often the precursor to something great, but it will always feel scary and lonely.

In my role now as an investor, I meet entrepreneurs every day who would love an investor to come on board with them to de-risk their venture. They are hoping someone else will risk their capital on their idea, and help soften the blow if things don't work out, making it possible to take big leaps with a big safety net underneath. Yet that's not how venture funding works. Capital is designed to propel risk-takers and enable them to take bigger leaps, not to provide safety nets in case you fall. Venture funding is fuel in your tank to enable you to do more of what you are already doing after you've proven you are on to something. It isn't a safety net.

Lori had to sell her home and give up her corporate income to create her minimum viable product before investors would consider backing her idea. We had to prove we had found product-market fit with a product that people wanted and were willing to pay for. Our own resources and those of our friends and family are often the resources we need first to test our ideas and start to bring things to life. That requires us to take big risks first.

I know many of us would argue "I just don't have the resources I need to make the leap. My family doesn't have any resources I can leverage. How can I make the leap without resources?" It's easy to get stuck in our heads, yet the reality is, it is unusual for any entrepreneur to have everything they need before they leap. That's what makes it a risk. So instead of just waiting for resources to be available to you or complaining that they are not available, ask yourself what you can do to make things happen and demonstrate that you believe in your idea. Can you get creative, just as I had to, with ways to fund your idea? I leveraged multiple credit cards, transferring balances between zero-interest cards. Could you find ways to start generating a small amount of revenue to give you a resource to generate more revenue?

Lisa Curtis, founder and chief executive officer (CEO) of Kuli Kuli Foods started her business with a crowdfunding campaign. After returning from the Peace Corps in Niger in 2011, she agreed to help her African colleagues build a market for moringa—a local superfood plant with incredible health benefits grown by rural women in Niger. She believed that moringa, just like goji berries, chia seeds, and quinoa, could become the next superfood craze that could also benefit the local African women she had been working with. An international market for their local product could be a game changer for that community and many across the region. And so, with deep conviction but only $2,000 in her bank account, she did what she could with virtually no money to create some small wins and build up her business to attract wider support and get her first investment.

Lisa started to experiment with moringa in her home kitchen, creating a batch of moringa bars. Realizing that the moringa powder had a strong flavor, she wanted to turn it into an easier-to-eat product, so bars became the first Kuli Kuli product. She quickly moved into a commercial kitchen. She spent her Saturdays gathering friends to help produce more bars so that they could go and sell them at farmers' markets the next day. She made smart bets by testing her newly created products and gathering data from her customers. She knew if she could get some hard data from her farmer's market crowd, understanding who was buying the product, what they liked about it, and what demographic they were, she could take that information to her local Whole Foods and demonstrate that she had a product people wanted and a specific group of people who would buy it. Over 16 percent of people who tested her product bought it, which is a strong percentage when compared to average sampling to purchase rates in the consumer-packed goods industry. Whole Foods Market Northern California said yes to this new product because she provided data. Before she even had a product that was commercially manufactured Whole Foods was willing to give her a shot. Her farmers' markets endeavors paid off, and the data she had collected enabled her to get her first big break.

Without the funding to properly manufacture her product, Lisa realized she had to give this idea everything she had. She quit her day job and started to look for as many sources of capital as she could. She launched a crowdfunding campaign in 2013, applied for grants, and she took a Kiva microloan to pay for the first run of bars for Whole Foods. She searched the world for the capital she needed to get started. Then she took to the road with her Kuli Kuli bars and launched her door-to-door sales campaign to convince grocery stores to start stocking her product. She spent hours passing out samples at each store that brought in Kuli Kuli bars. She knew that once people tried her product, they would buy it. Her sales began to drive growth, and just five months later she secured her first investment of $25,000 which quickly turned into a $500,000 seed round in 2014.

Kuli Kuli is now in eleven thousand stores across the US, is the largest moringa player in the world, and generates over $10 million in revenue a year. Lisa's start-small-but-go-all-in-and-get-creative approach paid off.

What do you need to do to double down on yourself? How do you need to shift your thinking to enable you to take big risks and go all in? Ask yourself what is holding you back. Remember, if you are not prepared to take risks on your idea, why would anyone else? If you aren't comfortable betting on yourself, it will be very hard to convince anyone else to bet on you.

The best risks I have ever taken have been when I've bet on myself to pull something off, to figure something out, or to make something happen. When I'm doubling down on myself, I show investors what I believe I'm capable of doing and that I'm willing to put my money, time, and energy where my mouth is. Not everyone needs to sleep in a camper with a three-year-old and nine-month-old in freezing conditions like I did. Not everyone needs to risk their home, or their life savings as Lori did, but you will likely need to get creative and demonstrate that you are comfortable making big leaps. The entrepreneurial journey will never cease to be risky, and investors know that people who make big things happen get good at taking risky leaps.

Creating Value

People who have created value before are more likely to be successful at scaling and growing a business. Creating value simply means having experience adding worth or significance to a product, service, or situation, which in turn enhances the satisfaction of customers, stakeholders, or society. Creating value often relates to your ability to contribute, provide unique solutions to problems, improve quality, increase efficiency, or deliver benefits that meet the needs and wants of the target audience. Many of us will have had previous careers where we contributed to the growth of another company or organization. Understanding our contributions and the abilities we brought to the table previously, which aided growth, is a testament to our capabilities to build something new of value. If we've created value before and know what adding value looks like, we're much more likely to have a broad range of skills that will enable us to create value in our new enterprise. Previous value creation is a great indicator of the potential capabilities of a budding entrepreneur.

Women who have had successful careers often write themselves off as not being entrepreneurial material because they don't look like your typical start-up founder. But not being able to make it onto the *Forbes* "30 Under 30" list doesn't negate your ability to build something great. Your previous experience might make you more likely to build something of great value. Your life and work experiences can be the right anchor to demonstrate why you are the perfect person to build your company and create something of extraordinary value for all stakeholders.

What previous experience have you had in making something happen that could be an indicator that you are a value creator, or even an indicator that you need to get into the entrepreneurial arena? Do you believe in your ability to add value while recognizing your unique talents and skills?

For Ayeshah Abuelhiga, CEO and founder of Mason Dixie Foods, her career history finally made her realize that she really was an entrepreneur and that she needed to start her own company. As a self-starter, she worked three restaurant jobs to put herself through college, then started working in consulting roles across industries, from Microsoft to Audi. Ayeshah quickly took on more responsibility in every role she had, consistently beating targets and outperforming her male colleagues. Yet she found she was constantly hitting glass ceilings, watching her less-experienced male colleagues be promoted before her. After fifteen years of working for other companies, she knew she would never reach the top if she waited for someone else to promote her. Her experience had taught her what she really knew deep inside all along—she was an entrepreneur. She knew she had created enormous value for other companies. Why not, then, build something she deeply cares about and create value for herself and her family by launching her own company?

Ayeshah launched Mason Dixie Foods in 2014, building on her parents' legacy of their carry-out restaurant and convenience store, with a vision to change comfort food for the better. Today, her frozen homestyle biscuits can be found in thousands of retail stores across the US and on the breakfast table at Marriott Hotels.

There was so much Ayeshah didn't know and so much learning still necessary, but she did know that she had the passion and drive within her to do something great. What had held her back from launching earlier? Her sense of responsibility and the expectations of her family meant that she needed to have a stable professional career, be a breadwinner for her family, and walk a traditional path. Yet she knew deep down that no matter how hard she worked at her career, she would never be rewarded sufficiently for the work she was prepared to do. Her desire to create value eclipsed the reward her employers were able to offer her. The moment Ayeshah realized that no matter how hard she worked for others, she would never be able to fully reap the benefits of the value she had created, she knew that she had to start building something of her own. This was the pivotal moment when Ayeshah knew she was a value-creator.

How have you created value for yourself or others in the past? What have you done previously to demonstrate to yourself and potential investors that you have what it takes to execute your vision and make big things happen? You don't need to have created massive value on a huge scale. The point, after all, is not about how much value you've created, but whether you understand what it means to create value and if you have the drive to build something big.

Selling You

This pitch deck is not only about selling your ideas, products, or services. The pitch deck is also selling you and your ability to create value, make things happen, and be tenacious. It is selling your willingness to go all in to build something great. You are the nucleus of it all. Selling yourself is just as critical as pitching your business concept.

Historically, women have not been as good as men at putting themselves forward and selling their capabilities and vision. Men are not necessarily better executors, value drivers, risk takers, or big business builders, but their willingness to recognize the value of networking and self-promotion has propelled them to the front of the line for funding.

Research has consistently shown that men apply for a job when they meet only 60 percent of the qualifications. Whereas women only apply when they meet 100 percent of the criteria.[3] Are women feeling less confident in their abilities than men? Author and women's coach Tara Sophia Mohr argues that that isn't the case. "What held [women] back from applying was not a mistaken perception about themselves, but a mistaken perception about the hiring process," says Tara. She insightfully recognizes that women see the playing field differently, believing they can only play when they believe they are qualified to do so and often underestimating what makes them qualified. However, men are much better at putting themselves in the arena and giving themselves a shot, regardless of whether they are qualified to be there. A sense of worthiness often plays a critical role in the way women can progress. Whether that's pitching for funding or applying for a job, men are more likely to make an application, to put themselves forward, and to toot their own horns than women. Men are much more likely to interpret the rules less as requirements and more as guidelines.

Women are also much more likely to believe in meritocracy. Our qualifications, after all, have historically been our way of proving that we could do the job. We have never been part of an old boys' network and have therefore tended to overestimate the importance of experience and formal qualifications and underestimate networking. The game of securing funding or gaining a promotion, for that matter, has much more to do with building relationships, proposing big plans, and selling yourself than ticking all the right boxes or having all the right experience.

Lisa Curtis remembers in her early days of getting funding, she was tempted to humbly present her ideas to transform Niger's rural communities as a charitable project to help Africa. When she realized that she had to step outside of her comfort zone, she began to show up at every networking event presenting her ideas as a multimillion-dollar opportunity to bring the next superfood to market. Lisa remembers having to shake off her humility and her small-mindedness about her project and reposition herself and her business as the next new superfood to hit the market that was going to be worth $1 billion. She saw a huge market opportunity, and with traction already at Whole Foods, her company had received some great coverage in the San Francisco Chronicle. Lisa had to learn to walk into every room communicating that she was going to be the next big thing in superfoods, not playing down her ideas but instead making big claims, sharing her big vision, and confidently declaring what she was going to do. "You have to have that level of confidence to make other people believe it," she says.

We tend to play down our ideas, not wanting to oversell anything and make big claims. But women must be bold, deliberate, and confident when we say, "I'm creating a whole new category of food in the market that doesn't exist right now." Or, "I'm building a whole new industry in the travel space. It's going to be worth billions, and I'm going to lead it." The glamping industry is expected to be worth $6 billion to the US economy by 2030 and is already contributing $3 billion globally every year.[4] My own company, Under Canvas, was the catalyst for creating this economic segment in the United States. Despite being repeatedly told over and over that "glamping is not a thing," I knew we could do something that no one else was doing. We knew we were the pioneers of a whole new industry. I needed to not be apologetic when communicating what we were doing, and I needed to stop approaching it like we were doing something small when we were out to do something big, even in the face of rejection.

We must believe in our ideas, and our lives should demonstrate that we believe in ourselves as we go all in, make sacrifices, and take big risks to demonstrate to the world that we are the value creators of the future. We need to paint clear pictures of what our businesses can be to the media, investors, and potential recruits so that other people can start to see what we see. We've got to get out there and sell ourselves as if our lives depend on it. Women must get better at entering the arena, whether we feel qualified or not, and toot our own horns while promoting ourselves and selling our unique capabilities. It is just like getting a new job—we will never get the job if we don't apply. We won't ever change the statistics on female funding if we don't believe that we are just as likely to succeed as our male counterparts. The data in this regard is even on our side. Research has shown that women-owned companies are more likely to generate higher revenues than those owned by men and that women are likely to make twice as much per dollar of investment as men.[5]

The rules of this game are not what we assume they are. Historical merit, experience, and qualifications are not the primary ingredients we need to be successful. Having drive and determination, being prepared to take big risks, making sacrifices to make things happen, and selling ourselves is what will get us noticed, because we will already be building scalable, impressive companies that are going places. You are the product investors are most interested in. Now you just need to believe and act like it.

Questions for Reflection

- How would you rate your tolerance for risk on a scale of 1–10?
- What leaps are you afraid to make? What holds you back?
- What have you sacrificed for your business to be where it is today? What big risks have you taken? How have you gone all in to get your business off the ground?
- How creative are you at finding the resources you need to help you make big leaps? What causes you to get stuck?
- How does your own sense of worth show up when you need to promote yourself? Are you selling yourself with a high degree of confidence and expectation?
- How could you sell yourself by demonstrating how great you have been at creating value before?

Slide Four of the Pitch Deck: The Product

On this slide, you are going to showcase your product or service. Provide images or an embedded video link to help us understand what your product looks like, what it does, and how it works. Help us really get a feel for your product or service. Just don't forget that you are also selling yourself!

4

Market Size Supersized

Every Big Dream is initially way beyond your abilities and experience. We all feel Unworthy and Unable to do a Big Dream.

—Bruce Wilkinson

One afternoon, toward the end of our grueling first summer in Yellowstone, exhausted and feeling half dead from the endless running around, long days and nights, and barely a day off in four long months, I found myself experiencing a rare moment alone in our camper. I love to journal, so with a fresh, hot cup of tea in hand, I started scribbling down all that had happened that summer. I recalled a huge snow dump in May that blanketed our camp overnight, leaving our guests, who had only brought shorts and T-shirts, heading to the nearest gift store. I remembered the afternoons when my three-year-old son would go off with one of our staff to do what he called "the trash run." His delight at riding the four-wheeler and going into each tent to empty the trash cans excited him to no end. Our dog Jasper regularly went off to play with a local coyote that would come by our camp. There was also the bison that wandered through our camp one day and acted like they owned the place, which Jasper the dog had a lot to say about until they charged him, and he scurried into the reception tent to hide behind me! There was the memory of getting up in the middle of the night when it was freezing to change the propane tank in order to keep our heat on and prevent the ice from forming inside our camper walls. And, of course, that infamous storm that almost finished me off. There were so many moments, good and bad, crazy and scary, but I realized that summer had changed our lives forever. Among all the exhaustion, I also felt excitement. The excitement that we were finally on to something. The excitement that we had something full of potential. It dawned on me as I was writing that we were also creating an extraordinary opportunity for ourselves. We could not only create one tented camp in Yellowstone, but we could create tented camps across the US. It became clear to me that our small business could scale and that if we could serve thousands of people each summer in one location, then we could potentially serve hundreds of thousands of people, maybe even millions, in tens of locations. I realized we could build something bigger than ourselves, and our vision suddenly got big.

I felt a sense of excitement, but also a sense of terror. I couldn't imagine going through the summer I had just gone through again. I could feel my stomach starting to tense. We looked worse for wear coming out of that first season. The amount of pressure both Jake and I had been under was intense on every level. Honestly, it was an amazing gift of grace that our marriage was still intact because we were overworked, exhausted, and overly stretched. We had pushed ourselves to the brink, but we also discovered our capacity to be resilient together. To this day, when times feel hard, we still look back at that time and say, "If we can survive Yellowstone, we can survive anything." This period forged something deep in us, cementing us together, defining and crafting new roles for each of us, and setting us on a path that would transform our lives and family forever. This was the moment we knew we had a big idea that could scale.

A few days later, while discussing our plans for next year, one of our staff asked, "Will you do this again?" I distinctly remember saying, "Yes, and I think we will start more of them."

He was baffled. "What?! Are you crazy? You're starting more?" he asked.

"Yes," I said. I could see that if this idea worked in Yellowstone, it could also work across the country. I realized we had something. We knew we had found product-market fit and had an amazing opportunity in front of us.

Present Over Perfect

Realizing that we were committed to exponential growth did not mean we fully understood or had reached the perfect version of Under Canvas; far from it. When I compare what we had back then to today's version of Under Canvas, it was terrible. But we asked ourselves, "Should we perfect our small camp until it's meticulous and flawless, and then try to replicate it? Or do we figure out how to perfect it as we go and build the plane while we are flying it?" We chose the latter option. We didn't wait to perfect what we had before we started to think about scale.

It is natural to want to perfect something before launching it for expansion, but thinking about scale and doing something much bigger from the outset changed the way we thought about building, resourcing, and managing the business. Up to that point, we had served three thousand to four thousand guests. Given how we started, that was a celebrated accomplishment for us. But when we changed our mindset and started to think like we were going to be a big company that would one day do tens of millions of dollars of revenue, that shifted our approach from thinking about doing everything ourselves to bringing in the expertise we needed to execute on a much larger scale. Thinking bigger changed the scope of what we were trying to do, and therefore, we had to shift our approach to building the company. We had to imagine it without us doing everything and quickly think about building a much more professional organization. I had to abandon the "it all depends on me" mindset that so many women struggle with and embrace the reality that if we were going on this new journey, we needed a great team of outstanding people around us. I knew I couldn't keep working the way I had been that past year and had to shift my thinking from doing everything myself to being the captain of a busy ship.

When Jake and I started the business together, we divided responsibilities based on our abilities, like many founders and small business owners. We both took on multiple roles. Jake was the brilliant inventor, designing and building all our meticulously crafted tents, infrastructure, and equipment while also overseeing the maintenance and functionality of our small camp. Meanwhile, I focused on driving sales, managing marketing efforts, and ensuring customer satisfaction. Our partnership thrived as we leveraged our skills for the company's success, and no doubt, without either of us, we would not have succeeded. However, as we contemplated scaling our business and team, we recognized the need to clearly define our roles and responsibilities.

Consequently, Jake took on the role of chief design officer, and I took on the role of chief executive officer. It was important that we and the team members around us knew who was doing what. Defining our roles brought a lot of clarity to the business and ourselves, especially as we started to assemble a diverse and skilled leadership team around us.

The ability to imagine your business running without you doing everything is a huge distinction between a small business and a small but scaling business. In a small business, everything revolves around the founder, who is responsible for everything, and all employees typically report to him or her. This, of course, limits the growth of the business to what the founder can handle. As soon as the founder is out of capacity, growth is stunted because they can't manage or do anymore. But in a business that is attempting to scale, operations no longer revolve around the founder. The founder or founders are no longer at the center of every-thing but instead become the strategists and visionaries, putting in place the people and building blocks needed for the business to function on a day-to-day basis without them. The founder's role is then less day-to-day and more tactical, bigger picture, business development focused, and usually becomes more defined into a specific area of business oversight.

That was our first major decision after deciding to scale our business. We knew that if we were going to grow and replicate what we had created, two things had to happen immediately. We needed to bring someone else on board to operate our existing tented hotel who had experience running hotels in order to free us up to start working on looking for new locations where we could open other camps.

Deciding to hire a chief operating officer (COO) was scary because, like most small businesses, we were operating on a shoestring and had no idea how we would pay for this expertise. Our first year in Yellowstone saw us make a very modest profit of a few thousand dollars (before paying ourselves anything), which certainly wasn't going to be enough to pay for the level of expertise we needed and cover all our costs between the end of one season and the start of the next. It seemed like an impossible task. Yet I've learned repeatedly over the years that where there is a will, there is always a way. There is usually a solution to every problem, particularly if we are prepared to be creative and resourceful.

Doug (name changed for anonymity), our first major hire, was a seasoned hotel operator and knew the hotel business inside out and back to front. He had decades of experience, was open to the challenge of operating a new kind of tented hotel, and, most surprisingly, was willing to take a chance on us. Creatively, he proposed a revenue share arrangement with us, which meant he would take a share of the revenue coming in, and we would both be rewarded if he could drive more revenue than we had when operating ourselves that first year. He believed he could take our idea and use his expertise to drive more revenue, make the operations more efficient, and, therefore, more profitable, and he would start to professionalize the business. His instinct wasn't wrong—that second year in Yellowstone looked completely different from the first in every way. For us, our business growth and evolution meant that I no longer had to live in a camper with two small children, working night and day. We leased a home in Bozeman, Montana, just an hour up the road from Yellowstone, and we established our business headquarters there in a small log cabin.

Making a big hire, though nerve-racking at the time, certainly paid off. Doug more than paid for himself, doubling our revenue in that second year, and with Doug at the helm of operations, this freed us up to work on growth. We quickly got to work scouring the country for our next camps, taking the children and dog on long road trips to look for land.

Being willing to bite the bullet and make bold decisions to recruit top talent is one of the foundational building blocks required to build a big business. Thinking about scale from the outset is the first step toward creating a business that could be investable. You need a dream that might seem crazy to others but that you can see clearly in your mind.

One of my all-time favorite films is *Field of Dreams*. Part of the magic of the film is the intrigue created by Kevin Costner, who sees what others cannot and decides to respond to a whisper he hears one day that says, "If you build it, they will come." Threatened by bankruptcy, Ray Kinsella, Costner's character, listens to the voice and vision he experienced. He plows his corn field and builds a baseball field without knowing its purpose. Once the field was built, baseball legends from the past mysteriously showed up to play ball.[1] The creation of the field evokes a magical sense of awe and wonder that I often felt in the early days of building Under Canvas. I sometimes found myself whispering the famous line, "If you build it, they will come," hoping and praying that guests would indeed come if we built what we could imagine in our dreams. We had a vision for something that did not exist yet—something we believed could be great, something others had not seen.

Our dreams should scare us; they should seem impossible to reach until we bring them to fruition. As Richard Branson reminds us, "If our dreams don't scare us, they are too small."[2] Feeling afraid of what we can imagine is a sure sign that we are moving in the right direction. We should see fear as a confirmation that we are finally beginning to think big enough! My vision was well beyond our limited financial resources, and the massive scale of what we were trying to accomplish terrified me. But instead of letting that fear paralyze us, we need to learn to harness that fear and allow it to empower us rather than hold us back.

Playing Safe

Women often want to play it safe. We think too small and limit ourselves by underestimating our capacities. We see this in the entrepreneurial space, with women often only pursuing lifestyle businesses, an arena that they've been conditioned to believe is what is achievable for and expected of them, rather than thinking about building big, scalable businesses. Yet, when we take off the parameters of that conditioning, it allows us to dream bigger and do more.

When my first son was born, I imagined I was supposed to stay home with him and focus all my attention exclusively on him and homemaking. My mother raised my sister and I that way. During my first two years as a mother, I helped my husband on the side with his business, but I thought of myself as a stay-at-home mom first. I hated not feeling like I was achieving anything each day and that my day had no challenges beyond entertaining an infant and fixing dinner. I experienced a crisis of confidence as I struggled to understand why I wrestled with my status as a stay-at-home mom.

The societal expectation that the burden of childcare should fall predominantly on women can swallow women whole. It's easy for women to feel held back or to hold themselves back out of guilt or fear that aggressively pursuing their dreams will somehow prevent them from being good mothers. Women are three times as likely as men to say that being a parent makes advancing their job or career harder.[3]

My father, who saw my struggle, said, "Sarah, you were not educated to stay home." I thought, "Oh? Right." I went to a competitive girls' grammar school in the UK, then earned a law degree and, subsequently, a master's degree. I hadn't acquired all that education to not extend or challenge myself. Don't misunderstand me: If you want to be a stay-at-home mom, I adamantly support your right to do so. But realizing I had a choice gave me permission to consider other options.

The unfortunate truth for many women is that we often feel like we need *permission*. We need permission to feel that it's okay to be who we are and follow our dreams. We need permission to imagine big futures for ourselves. We need permission to love our children while not wanting to be home with them all day every day. We have been living in a world where women look to others to give them permission to do things. But we have run out of time waiting for the world to grant us its blessing. If we are to create a more inclusive world, women must give themselves permission to go for it! Women are worthy, capable, educated enough, and just as good as our male counterparts. Plus, we have solutions and continue to solve problems men don't even know exist.

The challenges of simultaneously running a big business and raising children are not to be underestimated, but it is possible to navigate both worlds at the same time if we are willing to really listen to ourselves and our unique desires and accept help and support. I wanted to pursue having a family, and I wanted to be a successful entrepreneur, so I had to be creative in how I navigated juggling the combined roles of CEO and Mom. It took a willingness to create unique solutions that would work for our family and lifestyle, accept the support of others, and create a life that was not tied to a fixed schedule or place. In our early Yellowstone days, we had an au pair join our family to help look after our children, and later, we recruited an elementary school tutor to help educate our children as we traveled around the country building new camps. That additional external support enabled us to keep our family unit together, but I had to surrender to the idea that our life wasn't going to look like everyone else's. My children's school years were going to be different than most. I was not going to be able to be a traditional soccer mom or be able to show up at school for reading hour. I had to stop worrying about not being able to do what other moms did and had to focus on finding solutions to be able to do everything that I deemed important. "Mom guilt" definitely still shows up occasionally, as I inevitably can't do something my kids would love me to do or I feel like I should do. But I believe I've been more emotionally present and available for my children than if I'd stayed home with them constantly or taken a more traditional job. It's easy to make excuses and say something isn't possible, but you never know what is possible until you try. Don't let societal expectations or even your own frameworks limit what could be possible for you and your family.

What internal psychological parameters do you have to shift to move beyond your current limitations? What ceilings do you need to remove? Do you need to eliminate the necessity for perfection or complete order in your life and home before you can think big? Do you need to hear you have permission to dream bigger than anyone else you know? If so, please hear it. You don't need to be perfect; your ideas don't need to be polished into fine gemstones before you can get started. You have permission to imagine a future for yourself that no one else can quite grasp yet. You have permission to think one hundred times bigger than you already do. Believe in yourself, give yourself some credit, and go knock down those walls and burst through those ceilings. Imagine what our world might look like if a few more of us did just that.

We ended our first season in Yellowstone exhausted but with a brand-new vision for the future in which we could imagine not just one tented hotel, but many. A vision that would propel us forward in ways we could not have imagined at the time but which would help us build a big business.

Large Markets

Business ideas that can be built into something huge all have one thing in common: they always address large markets that have the potential to reach over a billion dollars in value. The "B" word is intimidating, but remember that a large market does not necessarily mean you must build a company worth a billion dollars. Instead, it is your idea that must be big enough to reach millions of people in a market that could be worth more than a billion dollars. As I previously mentioned, the global glamping market is currently worth $3 billion annually and is estimated to reach $6 billion in the United States alone by 2030. Market size, therefore, simply represents how big something could be.

The fourth slide of the pitch deck is about communicating to investors the scale of your idea and vision. The three metrics used to measure the magnitude of an idea and the size of a market are total addressable market (TAM), serviceable addressable market (SAM), and serviceable obtainable market (SOM).

Total Addressable Market

First, let's start by communicating the total size of the market. The total addressable market (TAM) reflects the potential of your vision and how big the whole market is. If you imagined starting a chain of family restaurants across the United States, for example, you would tell us the total size of the restaurant market in the United States. Market size comprises the total number of potential buyers of a product or service within a given market and the total revenue that these sales may generate. The fastest way to find this information is to search for the required statistics on Google. Google said the chain restaurant sector was expected to reach $50 billion in 2022.

The TAM gives us a sense of whether your business vision is one with lots of room for growth and huge potential. It allows us to assess whether your business could contribute to a large market and whether you could capture a piece of this market. Investors are interested in how big of a market your idea is addressing. Is the audience for your product or service made up of hundreds of thousands, even millions of people, or just you and five of your friends? Could the market you are creating or operating within be worth over $1 billion?

Let's say they are selling lipstick in the US market. You would then communicate to your potential investors the total size of the US cosmetic industry, valued at approximately $90 billion in 2020. This metric communicates to your investors that your business idea has huge potential as it addresses a big, valuable market already worth over a billion dollars.

Thinking about your TAM is easier with business ideas in markets that already exist. What happens if your category or your market doesn't yet exist or if you are creating something totally new? Then you need to think more laterally. When we started Under Canvas, the glamping industry did not yet exist; there were no statistics about the value of the glamping market. However, the adventure travel market did exist. So, we could leverage the growing statistics around adventure travel that demonstrated that adventure travel was a large market that was increasing in growth and spending. If you can't find relevant dollar statistics, you could also use consumer numbers. For example, 100 million people participate in adventure travel-related activities each year. However, describing your TAM in dollars would certainly be preferable if you could source data relevant to your business. Addressing the TAM for your investors makes it easy for them to quickly see the value of your market arena.

Gathering this data takes time and energy, but well-thought-through data is an asset you bring to the table, showing the investor (and yourself) that you have done your research and understand the potential value of the market you are addressing. Being able to talk about how this market is growing or what is expected to happen in this space is also extremely useful. A growing market, for example, increases confidence and interest.

Serviceable Addressable Market

The next step is to break down the TAM and communicate your serviceable addressable market (SAM), which is the specific niche within the overall market you will address. Your SAM is a portion of the TAM targeted by your specific products and services within your geographical reach. Taking the same cosmetic example above, if you had lipstick as your product, we would calculate the size of the lipstick category ($1.6 billion in 2020) as a portion of the overall cosmetic industry. That would give us a TAM of $90 billion and a SAM of $1.6 billion. The SAM is how big the market is for your specific products or services within your geographical reach and communicates the big picture, or total market size, for your specific niche.

Serviceable Obtainable Market

The SAM for your business is then broken down one last time by determining how much of the SAM we believe our business can obtain. This final step calculates the actual size of your specific business, or your serviceable obtainable market (SOM). Out of the total market for lipsticks of $1.6 billion annually, your SOM is a piece of that market that you believe your business will capture. For example, you might say your SOM will be $100 million, which would be 6.25 percent of the lipstick market, or SAM. Your SOM is arguably the data point that matters the most because it communicates succinctly, in one number, how much revenue you think your business could ultimately do. Projecting this number takes thought, wisdom, and the ability to think big, but at the same time, must be grounded in believable facts. Your SOM number as a percentage of your SAM cannot be too high—you can't try and convince anyone that you are going to become 50 percent of the serviceable market—but you also can't think too small either. As Goldilocks would encourage us, we're looking for a number that is just right. As we contemplate what just right looks like, there are several factors we need to consider.

Big Enough

Investors are looking for ideas that can scale, and that could ultimately be worth millions of dollars. Does your business idea have the capability of being big enough? The goal is to present your business's scalability and to demonstrate that you are building a business that could be valuable enough to warrant an investment. Just how big is big enough?

I recently heard a pitch from a fantastic founder who had the vision for digitizing vehicle licensing in South Africa. Digitizing services in Africa is a much-needed endeavor, and I loved the look of the online platform, which was easy to use and navigate. The ability to ensure that patrons' vehicle registration was renewed quickly and efficiently was also fantastic. The company had great traction, with numerous users flooding to the site to avoid standing in line to renew their vehicle registrations by choosing to complete the process online instead. However, when I started to dig into the market size, the pitch started to fall apart. The total SAM was only the twelve million cars on South Africa's roads, which sounds like a lot of vehicles, but the quick back-of-the-envelope math demonstrated that the market wasn't large enough to invest in. If 100 percent of the market was twelve million cars, that meant the total size of the market was only worth approximately two hundred million dollars based on the seventeen-dollar fee per registration they would charge for each renewal or first-time license. If every car owner in the country used the service, the total amount of revenue that could be generated would be two hundred million dollars ($17 x 12 million cars = approximately $200 million). Knowing the company would only ever capture a small percentage of car owners each year due to competition from other online providers and that only a certain percentage of people would choose to renew online versus in person, it quickly became clear the total market size was too small. We imagined the SOM to potentially be no more than 5 percent of the SAM, which would equate to ten million dollars in revenue. I encouraged the founder to look at expanding to other markets in Africa to offer the same service or to think about incorporating other types of licensing renewal on the platform, TV license renewal, for example. Knowing that government services in Africa desperately need to be digitized, I encouraged thinking bigger than the niche the company was currently working in, as the current market parameters felt too small. The vehicle licensing market in South Africa alone was not a big enough market. However, incorporating Botswana, Zambia, Namibia, and the Democratic Republic of the Congo could sufficiently enlarge the market. Similarly, expanding the types of renewal services that could be offered to the sixty million people of South Africa, could also increase market size.

This founder needed to think bigger and make the necessary shift in mindset around scale and possibilities, in order to not impact the ability to raise capital and grow the business. Interestingly, despite the advice, this founder struggled to think bigger, partly because they felt they had to start implementing all that new potential growth right away and partly because they struggled to see how it would be actually possible to offer new online registrations. They didn't feel ready to start expanding to new regions or to implement other licensing opportunities. Certainly, those ideas could have remained growth opportunities for a later date that did not need to be implemented or figured out right away. But they could not get comfortable presenting a vision today that was large enough to invest in. The founder needed to inspire confidence that the market they were thinking about addressing was big enough to drive significant revenue—revenue that would, in turn, drive a return for the potential investor. Ideally, this founder would have presented a TAM worth well over $1 billion, including various licensing opportunities across Africa. That their specific geographical reach would offer services in four or five countries and that the SOM could be worth at least $100 million.

Lack of confidence and thinking they had to have workable solutions right away meant they shied away from the possibility of increasing the scope and scale of the business. The inability to think bigger not only hindered the ability to gain investment but also to capture a larger share of the market. This market is now saturated with competitors, many of whom are now providing services beyond vehicle registration renewals.

What does big enough look like? In recent years, tech companies and their lofty valuations have skewed our ideas of what big looks like. We don't need to build billion-dollar companies to have built big companies. Still, I do believe a good benchmark is to ask yourself if the niche your business operates in, your SAM, could be worth over a billion, and therefore, could your business, your SOM, be worth one hundred million. For venture capital funding purposes, I'm defining "big" as creating a company that could be worth $100 million or more. If our vehicle license entrepreneur had demonstrated a SAM worth a billion dollars, it would have been much easier to think about investing, knowing that they could capture a share of that market and build a business worth $100 million or more.

Too Good to Be True

In contrast to underselling yourself, we've all experienced moments when something sounds too good to be true, such as adverts for weight loss products or programs, that promise huge amounts of miraculous weight loss, or used car salespeople trying to convince you that a car with 500,000 miles (about 804,672 km) on the clock is really in outstanding shape. We all know the feeling we get when we are told information that just does not sound believable. Investors can also feel hoodwinked when you present numbers that do not land in the realm of the feasible.

Part of the struggle with defining your SOM is ensuring your numbers make sense and that there is a methodology behind your reasoning. It isn't enough to simply sell the idea that you are going to capture 1 percent of the market and make one hundred million dollars in revenue. Is there a plan to back your numbers up? On what basis are you making your assumptions?

Start by working backward from your end revenue goal and asking your-self what it would take to make that much revenue. How many customers would you need? How many products would you need to sell? How many locations would you need if you had a multi-site business like I had? Then, work backward from those numbers, determining what you'd need to do each year to finally reach that ultimate revenue number. How many years might it take to get there? Ideally, it shouldn't take longer than ten to twelve years. Factor in how easy it will be to market to acquire those customers. Is there pent-up demand for your product or service, or will you need to create demand, which will take time and money? Will you have any restrictions or barriers, such as competition, geographical challenges, or production capacity? What are the factors that will influence how easy it will be to generate revenue? You might discover, like our vehicle license founder, that it's impossible to generate enough revenue from only one revenue stream—so what other rev-enue streams would you need to bring in? Complete your analysis thoroughly and thoughtfully to ensure your metrics are as accurate as they can possibly be. That will help convince potential investors that you know what you are talking about, that you've carefully thought about your growth strategy, and that you have not underestimated how hard it will be to do what you are pro-posing. Presenting a thoughtfully contemplated strategy that convinces you that you are on to something big will also help convince others to believe you, too.

I hear pitches from entrepreneurs all the time who pull their SOM numbers out of thin air. When questioned about where and how they obtained that number, they fall apart because they haven't tactically thought through what it would real-istically take to pull off that amount of revenue or capture that segment of the market. They pitch a huge market share by arbitrarily guessing the percentage of the market they are going to capture. They spoil a great pitch by being unbeliev-able and ill-prepared to back up their claims with data.

There is no fixed way to determine your SOM; there are many ways you can approach it. It is often as much art as science, but having substance behind the conclusions you draw is required. In our above example, if we had started with a big enough addressable market, we could have calculated the potential of all the different licensing streams, making a good argument for how many people we could shift to renewing online. We calculated our SOM for Under Canvas based on how much revenue we believed we could generate from each location and how many locations we believed we could open within a ten-year time frame. That gave us some weighty numbers backed by substance that, in turn, projected that we were planning to build a big business and capture a sizable portion of a new market in the adventure travel space.

Why Does This Data Matter?

The specifics of whether or not you can deliver exactly what you've outlined in your market sizing slide are not what are critical to the investor at this point. Investors are looking to see if you have a big vision and a big enough market for investors to get their return on investment, or ROI. The sole purpose of your pitch to an investor is to help them spot an excellent entrepreneur operating in an exceptional niche that can generate an incredible yield on investment. The TAM, SAM, and SOM quickly help an investor evaluate the upside and risk associated with an opportunity. Each data point provides a baseline for investors to compare one opportunity with another and analyze the short- (three years), mid- (seven years), and long-term (ten to twelve years) growth potential. The SOM to SAM ratio describes the market share initially aimed for, and the TAM shows the greatest possible market potential.

I remember when the female venture capitalist (VC) who stayed at our camp told me the type of returns venture capitalists were looking for from their investments. The visibility around those numbers helped me think entirely differently about my business and what I would need to do to demonstrate not only how my business could meet those return metrics but also how I could drive returns by efficiently using investment capital to drive growth.

As a rule of thumb, early-stage venture capitalists are looking for a minimum return of ten times their investment and even higher if your business is in an emerging market like Latin America or Africa. If a VC invests $100 thousand, they are hoping to turn their investment into a minimum of $1 million. That means their share of the business would become worth $1 million. By doing some basic math, therefore, you can calculate if your SOM is going to be large enough for a VC to make the desired return on their investment. If you are projecting your SOM as $10 million and you are asking for $500 thousand in seed capital, you would quickly be able to see that the VC would need to own 50 percent of your company to achieve their desired return. No one would normally give 50 percent of their company away to an early-stage investor, so your SOM is likely too small. Early-stage investors typically take anywhere from a five to twenty-five percent stake in your fledging company, investing anywhere from several hundred thousand dollars up to $2 million. You, therefore, need to project that you have a big enough SOM to make an investment worthwhile, while remembering that you may also have several rounds of investors, not just one. Every investor at every stage will need to make a return. Later investors, who take less risk but who typically write larger checks, do often have lower return expectations, two or three times their money as opposed to the ten times of early-stage VCs. However, as a frame of reference, it is important to demonstrate that you are playing in a big market and that your business idea has the potential to create hundreds of millions of dollars in revenue.

You need a vision of what you intend to build and enough confidence to believe that if you launch your idea, customers will come. Are you ready to think bigger than you've ever imagined before? Are you ready to expand your mind to explore the possibility of figuring out if there is a pathway to one hundred million dollars for your business? Our vehicle licensing entrepreneur couldn't imagine how they could deliver online renewals for other license types, so they didn't want to commit to enlarging the market. Yet, without thinking big enough, they inadvertently relegated the business back into a small business box, stifling the ability to grow and raise capital. It takes enormous vision and courage to imagine what has not yet been done.

We grasped a big vision for Under Canvas, imagining our tented hotels across the country. Discovering a business model that had the potential to scale and seeing we had product market fit, even though it wasn't perfected yet, gave us the confidence to think big. Ultimately, thinking big launched us off on an entirely new journey that would change the trajectory of our business and our lives. Will thinking bigger change your trajectory, too?

Questions for Reflection

- What is holding you back from thinking big? What mindset is getting in your way?
- Do you need to think bigger still to build something big enough? What would happen if you imagined something one hundred times bigger than what you are currently thinking? What would that business look like?

- Spend some time working out your TAM, SAM, and SOM. Is your SOM large enough for a venture capitalist to jump in and back your business? Can you see a path to one hundred million dollars in revenue?
- What's the ratio between your SAM and SOM? Does that feel just right?

Slide Five of the Pitch Deck: Market Size

On this page, you want to present your TAM, SAM, and SOM data, making it easy for the investor to quickly see the headline numbers. You will want to qualify in smaller print what each number represents. For example, "the size of the cosmetic industry in the United States." Clarifying information helps us quickly discern how you arrived at those numbers. You could also add any growth trends that are relevant to your market or projections about how the market is expected to grow in the next five to seven years. Remember, you are trying to create confidence that you are operating in a big market and that you have the potential to make significant amounts of revenue.

Revenue and the Metrics That Matter

Because when you speak a language, English, well many people understand you, including Afrikaners, but when you speak Afrikaans, you know, you go straight to their hearts.

—Nelson Mandela

On a Thursday afternoon, four years after that monumental first summer in Yellowstone when the storm had nearly destroyed our business, I had flown down to San Francisco from Bozeman, Montana, to meet with potential investors. Our business had grown, and we now had three tented hotels: one in Yellowstone, one in Glacier National Park in Montana, and one in Moab, Utah. Each one had taken a massive amount of effort and energy to open, but our hard work was starting to pay off. We had started winning awards for our groundbreaking tented camps. Then, a chance meeting with another female entrepreneur at the Sunset Magazine Travel Awards ceremony propelled our business into another arena. Ruzwana Bashir, chief executive officer (CEO) and cofounder of Peek.com, was giving a keynote speech and sharing her own story of raising capital for her travel business, for which she had recently raised twenty-five million dollars. Knowing she knew more than I did about raising capital, I introduced myself after she finished sharing her story. Her enthusiasm and exuberance abounded, and she did not hesitate to open her network of investors to me by making half a dozen introductions, which changed the tide from endless "noes" to "let's meet." In the months leading up to that encounter, I had been having introductory calls with investors, many of whom had rejected me out of hand as

I wasn't building a tech company. Finally, here was someone who could introduce me to investors who were interested in the travel industry.

A few months after that encounter, I stepped into a San Francisco office, nervous but excited to talk to people who finally understood my industry. I was armed with my pitch deck and ready to give my presentation and tell our story so far.

Midway through my presentation, the venture capitalist (VC) asked me, "What's your CAC?" as he flipped through the pages of my deck. I looked blankly at him, suddenly wondering if I was in the wrong room. I honestly had no idea what he was talking about. He persisted: "Your cost of acquisition? What is it?"

"To acquire what?" I asked innocently.

He rolled his eyes, indicating I was wasting his time. "Customers. What does it cost you to acquire customers?"

I still couldn't directly answer the question. I fumbled my way through the question, explaining how we marketed our business with virtually no spending on advertising because I had listed our properties on Trip Advisor, Expedia, and Booking.com. I also explained how our revenue had been rapidly growing and that we believed glamping was the biggest new trend to hit the travel space.

The meeting was over before it had even begun. I never really got into my stride simply because the acronyms flung around the room by these potential investors were utterly unfamiliar. We were coming from parallel universes, and I left the meeting feeling frustrated and embarrassed, realizing for the first time just how much I did not yet know. The silver lining of these early failed investor meetings was realizing just how much I still had to learn. I discovered that every conversation I had was an opportunity to learn information that would be critical to growing my business. Could I quickly harness the knowledge gathered in these embarrassing conversations? Could I level up and learn the language I needed, not only to be able to communicate properly with investors but also to get someone to put capital into our business? Could I shift my sense of inadequacy and broaden my understanding of the value of my own business?

Learning Fast

I have learned over the last decade that a founder's ability to learn fast, as well as fail fast, is one of the key anchors that will determine how fast a company can grow. Your personal growth, your ability to learn, evolve, discover, and transform, and the speed at which you can do these things are connected to the growth and speed of your business's evolution. That's a scary thought, but the good news is that our personal growth and ability to learn are things that we can control. We can't control who will say "yes" to us out in the world, but we can commit to being quick studies and nimble enough to learn fast. The journey of growing a company is like being on a perpetual vertical learning curve. If the curve isn't steep, it is likely that we aren't learning new things quickly enough and are therefore hindering our company's growth.

I knew that if I could commit to learning fast, I could master the alien language of the world of venture capital. Sadly, I learned the hard way, but I wrote this book so you don't have to. Let's break down some of the most important acronyms that will fuel your learning curve and keep you from seeming as ignorant as I did when I first started pitching investors.

The Inherent Value of a Business

I had been on my entrepreneurial journey for several years before I realized that businesses themselves are valuable entities that can be bought and sold, rather than merely producing products or services that are bought and sold. It sounds so obvious now, but it certainly wasn't obvious to me at the time. From an extremely basic viewpoint, I knew businesses should make money by generating income minus expenses, which would in turn leave me with some profit as the difference. This rudimentary understanding of business was the extent of my comprehension of how businesses generate capital.

I never went to business school and had not been exposed to business growing up. My mum worked as a school librarian, and my father worked as a leader in local government. After I graduated from university, I went to work for a Christian non-profit organization in Zimbabwe, teaching AIDS education in schools and doing local youth work. Up until that point, my exposure to business was non-existent; my view of capitalism consisted of a worldview where massive capital generation involved going to the "dark side." Money was the root of all evil. I had never previously considered the possibility that building a business could be a force for good in the world or that a business could drive innovation, solve problems, create solutions to real obstacles, and in turn become valuable entities that do well and do good at the same time.

Once I realized that creating profit and doing good didn't need to be mutually exclusive, I knew I had an amazing opportunity to build something of real significance and impact. I had to shift my small-mindedness and short-term thinking and go all in with building something that could really do some good. I had to stop thinking about short-term profitability and financial survival and start thinking about building something of long-term value and significance. Not only did I have to start thinking bigger than I ever had before, but I had to begin to master an understanding of the financial metrics that were going to matter in my business. Knowing and understanding the data points that matter in our business helps us build a better, bigger business and will also help us know and speak the language investors use.

I remember the first time someone explained to me the definition of earnings, before interest, taxes, depreciation, and amortization (EBITDA), I was lost. Yet, this data point measures the overall financial performance of your business. It is a standard accounting metric that, in simple terms, is your net income or profit. The amount of money you make after all your expenses are deducted. EBITDA is a major indicator of the overall profitability of a business and is often the number upon which a business is valued. A multiple of your EBITDA number is what buyers will use to determine the value of your business. Together with your revenue number, EBITDA is the most significant number in your business. Knowing your EBITDA number and how that number is trending and growing over time is critical to demonstrating how your business is growing and therefore increasing in value.

When I realized that EBITDA was a significant metric and that recording my EBITDA trends over time was the pivotal element that would allow me to build value in my business, I realized I had to focus on this metric and look at how I could improve my EBITDA number in the business. I sought to optimize the business by managing our costs and driving growth in the form of adding new locations to our group. Every decision I made in the business, I considered through the lens of how that decision would affect our EBITDA over time. Would a short-term EBITDA dip be beneficial if it caused bigger growth in the long-term? With early-stage companies, investors often expect to see what is called "hockey stick" EBITDA growth, which is an initial dip (lower EBITDA) as the company invests in hiring the people and infrastructure needed for growth. Then a rapidly rising EBITDA number as the investments you have made in growth start to come to fruition. Knowing that short-term losses are expected and often inevitable in the near term made me less afraid of those losses and more willing to accept and plan for them, knowing we were building the capacity for growth in the future.

I could model out how our investments in one year would pay off in the next and beyond.

Understanding that the specific metric of EBITDA mattered affected the way I thought about and planned our growth trajectory. As I understood what was expected for a fast-growing company, I was able to think about growth on that trajectory and measure and track not only this metric but many other metrics that mattered in my business. Once I understood the metrics driving my business and began tracking them, I was able to make better, more informed decisions and strategically plan our growth to create value. Gaining a broader understanding of the fact that your business itself can be worth notably more than the income it produces today gives you the freedom to create that value by wielding your newfound knowledge of the key metrics driving your business.

The revenue page of the pitch deck is all about communicating your revenue model and significant metrics, as well as the building blocks that indicate whether you are building a valuable business or not. On this page, we get to tell a story about our business through data and numbers. Understanding these metrics and their complexity as they relate to your business is imperative to help you build better businesses and confidently point out your most valuable data insights and trends to your potential investors.

Proficiency in your business' metrics will not only enable your business to grow, but it will also set you apart from your competition and allow potential investors to determine whether it is viable for them to invest in your business.

Cost of Customer Acquisition

As I have already shared my embarrassing encounter over this data point, let's start here. Your cost of acquisition tells us how much it costs to acquire a new customer. To calculate this number, take your sales and marketing expenses and divide them by the number of new users or customers acquired: sales and marketing expenses divided by the number of new customers = customer acquisition cost.

Your sales and marketing expense number represents the internal and external expenses directly and indirectly related to selling and marketing your product or service. When calculating this number, make sure you include all your sales and marketing expenses, including the expenses of your marketing person who built your digital ads, your public relations (PR) team, and the person who answers customer service calls, as well as the actual spend on digital marketing. Include everything that you would categorize as your whole marketing and sales expenditure, then divide it by your paying customers that month or that year. Your cost of customer acquisition (CAC) indicates how difficult or easy it is to get people to use your product or services and how much money is needed to convince someone to use your service or buy your product. It is an important metric that tells you that if it costs more to acquire a customer than they spend with you, your business model may not be sustainable, and massive growth may not be possible.

In the early days of a business, it is common for the cost of acquisition to be proportionately high, but over time, investors expect to see your CAC go down as an overall percentage of your total revenue. It can take a lot of time, energy, effort, and spending to discover your marketing channel and sales formula of choice. Initially, your costs are likely to be high until you discover a highly scalable acquisition channel with a relatively low overall cost. The faster you can figure out the marketing channel that will work best for your business, the faster you will be able to get your CAC number down. Ultimately, if you cannot find a scalable channel you can invest in, it is going to be hard to scale what you are doing. For example, something that's hard to market (like our events business) didn't have a scalable channel to drive sales, which made it impossible to scale. Without a marketing channel that consistently works for your business, you either don't have product-market fit (a product that consumers want and are prepared to pay for in significant numbers) or your business is not yet scalable. Scalability is having a product or service that you can significantly grow or expand.

Retention

Investors understand that acquiring customers is an expensive and difficult exercise, so they like to frame a business in the context of how well the founder can retain their customers once acquired. In other words, does someone stay or continue to pay on an ongoing basis? How often are they using your service or buying from you? How much data are they giving you by transacting with you each time? There are lots of ways to think about retention, but retention is a key factor in building a customer base. Can you increase your retention over time? Can you increase your customers' spending? Can you increase frequency? When we started Under Canvas, our retention was incredibly low; guests stayed with us once on one trip, and that was it. Over time, our guests began to stay with us multiple times, often several times a year. What had changed for us? We had built multiple locations, allowing our guests to travel with us to different places. They stayed once and liked the experience and then stayed at another location and then another and another—they did not necessarily come back to the same location, but they were prepared to visit different locations. The more locations we had, the easier it became for our business to retain customers.

We need to look at our products and services and decide what retention we are trying to achieve. What would great retention look like in your business? What do you want your customers to do, ideally? With what frequency do you want people to use your business? How would your ideal customer behave? If we know what our ideal is and where our starting point is, we can then start to work on how we change our customers' behaviors and begin tracking those trends over time. We need to track retention, asking ourselves, "Am I changing or improving my retention or my repeat business over time?"

One of the reasons customer retention is so important is that it helps to bring the cost of acquiring new customers down. If you can sell more to the same customer base or keep your customers with you, you need to bring in fewer new customers to replace the customers you lost. Retention is like plugging a leaky bucket. You want to keep in your business what it costs you to acquire.

Investors want to understand what your retention numbers look like today and how much you can increase that retention level over time. They don't want to see a leaky bucket where you bring your customers in at the top and lose them at the bottom. The loss of clients is called *churn*. In other words, churn is the number of lost bookings or users who were once active. Churn is the antithesis of growth, and if your churn rate is high, that is a big indicator that you are on a downward trajectory.

Lifetime Value of your Customer

Connected to both our CAC and retention numbers is our lifetime value of your customer (LTV). This reflects the average amount that your business can expect to receive from a customer over their lifetime with you. The LTV would be the average total amount of money that you would expect a customer to spend with you, and it is impacted by how long they do business with you and how many transactions they do.

If we go back to our retention ideals for a moment, we might say our ideal customer buys products from us four times a year, spends $100 on each occasion, and continues to shop with us for five years. The lifetime value of that customer would be $4 \times 100 \times 5 = \$2,000$. In a software business, your ideal customer might pay $15 a month and stay on your platform for at least three years. That customer would be worth $15 \times 12 \times 3 = \$540$. To calculate this number, you need to know the average amount your ideal customer pays you in a transaction and how long they keep paying you. This can be challenging to calculate in the initial stages of monetization since there is not likely to be enough data to support the calculation, in which case you will be forced to make reasonable assumptions based on what you are expecting your LTV to be and adjust as you gather more data. Making assumptions, however, will start to allow you to look at your LTV and your CAC in conjunction with discovering the ratio between the two. If it costs you more than your LTV to acquire a customer, you know you have a problem. Ideally, you are looking for your LTV to be more than three and a half times your CAC, and you would expect your CAC to decrease and your LTV to increase over time.

A crucial component of this metric is to develop ongoing ways for your customers to continue spending money with you once you have acquired them, so that they remain with you for a long time and spend more money with you. A higher LTV will not only increase your revenue but will also ultimately enable you to build a more valuable company. How could you increase the LTV of your customer? What other products or services could you offer your customer? Could you increase the length of time they do business with you?

Monthly Recurring Revenue and Annual Recurring Revenue

Investors love start-ups with recurring revenue because there is a high degree of predictability and a low amount of churn. The same customer buying from you every month or every year would generate recurring revenue. Subscription businesses such as a subscription box, Software as a Service (SaaS) businesses, education platforms, gym memberships, and streaming platforms often have recurring monthly revenue. If we pay a monthly or annual subscription fee to use the service, the revenue becomes recurring (monthly recurring revenue

[MRR] and annual recurring revenue [ARR]). Not all business models generate monthly recurring revenue and that is perfectly fine. My own business did not, but instead, I would often be asked about repeat guests. Investors were looking for some associated retention metrics to confirm there would be some sort of recurring connection to a customer once we had acquired them. The more your business is recurring or repeating in nature, the more confidence it inspires in potential investors. The more regularity there is with repeat revenue, the better.

Growth Rate

Even more attractive to investors than recurring revenue is your growth rate, or how fast you are growing month-over-month or growing annually. The faster you are growing, the more attractive your company will be. I recently heard from a VC who gets pitched daily by early-stage entrepreneurs that a 10 percent month-over-month growth rate would not make him interested enough in the business to take a meeting with the founders. With 20 percent month-over-month growth, he might be interested, and at 30 percent he would take the meeting, but with a 50–100 percent month-over-month growth rate, he would be clearing the decks, emptying his schedule, and rolling out the red carpet for you. Understanding these figures helps us understand what we are competing against when we send our pitch decks to investors. Of course, not all investors have the same parameters, but knowing what outstanding growth looks like helps us put our own endeavors in context and should help us recognize what level of growth is going to be necessary to pique an investor's interest.

Every investable business is going to have a significant growth trajectory. This should remind us to think more aggressively about how we approach growth and remind us of how necessary it is to think big and create rapid growth. I didn't have a tech business, which we often imagine is the only kind of business that grows very rapidly. But that isn't true—all kinds of businesses can grow rapidly and be investable if they have sufficient scalability and the potential to grow rapidly. Under Canvas was a capital-intensive, real estate-based business, which was very different from the tech businesses that venture capital typically invested in. But Under Canvas was able to achieve extraordinarily rapid growth, and capital will always flow where there is a trajectory of rapid growth. Figuring out how to put yourself on that trajectory is, therefore, key.

Cash Burn

Burning money never sounds good, and it isn't, but it is inevitable in the initial stages of any business. Your *cash burn*, or the total amount of money you are consuming monthly, is the amount of cash you spend on operating activities plus the cash you spend investing in the growth of the business each month. Until you reach profitability, you will continue to burn cash. The obvious additional question investors will frequently ask is, "What does your path to profitability look like?" Determining how many months of cash burn you will have before you become profitable tells you how much cash the business will need to raise from outside sources and how many customers will be needed to cover all the expenses. Being able to demonstrate a pathway to becoming profitable and knowing how long that might take will lessen the impact of your cash burn and will make your business more robust overall. The faster your business can become profitable, the less time your business will be at the mercy of investors. Not being reliant on raising capital to keep your business alive will also ensure your business can withstand tough economic times, market downturns, and the fragility of the investment world.

Tracking and understanding these key metrics will not only be important for investors but will also be critical for you to see what is happening in your business. Looking at your data, knowing your data, and tracking your data gives you a clear understanding of the performance of your business and an indication of existing problems. Data on your business tells you what you need to be working on, what is working and what's not, and which aspects of your business are going to scale and which are not. Once you get past the idea stage of your business and you've started to grow, your metrics will be the biggest indicator of whether you have a potential runaway success or not.

Impact Metrics

In a world where data is everything, having great financial performance metrics is critically important. However, in addition to these metrics, there's one additional way you can use data to help you stand out. You can differentiate your business by also including environmental, social, governance (ESG) metrics, or impact metrics, to ensure your business stands out from the crowd. Impact metrics can be your data on how you are doing good in the world. For example, your environmental credentials or your socioeconomic impact. You shouldn't lead with your impact metrics, as your financial performance and projections should be your compelling hook, but the good your business can do could be just the thing that makes your business stand out and capture the hearts and minds of your audience. Investors are often looking for investments that not only align with their investment strategy but also resonate with their interests and passions, and these metrics help them connect with why you are building your company. It becomes a compelling proposition for potential investors to discover that by investing in a business that also creates good in the world, they are themselves positively impacting the world with their capital.

When we launched Under Canvas, we aimed to help preserve and protect some of the most beautiful places in the United States. We knew traditional development typically heavily impacted the land, usually leveling it and rebuilding it from scratch, removing every native species. We wanted to prove that we could develop a hotel without having to destroy the land we wanted to protect. So, we built tented hotels that used one-tenth of the water of a same-size traditional hotel and that used very minimal electricity. This meant the bathrooms in our tents used low-flow fixtures and fittings, saving a considerable amount of water. Our camps typically also ran off solar power, so we limited the use of electricity in the camp. We also wanted to leave no trace, so that if we ever ceased trading, we could pack up the hotel and ensure the landscape would look almost untouched and unchanged. We wanted to preserve the natural feel of the wilderness we were inhabiting, creating access to it without producing highly manicured, water-intensive resort-like landscaping. We wanted to help people get back to nature and experience the power of the great outdoors. Our big "why" for building this business was to impact people's lives. Over the last twenty years, I have become a passionate believer in the power of the outdoors to make us healthier, both mentally and physically, and to make us more productive by giving us the space and time we need to think, have big ideas, and be creative. I wanted to create opportunities for others to travel in experiential ways, to explore, to be immersed in nature, and, in turn, to become more responsible and care about our planet. When we are out in nature, it is hard not to recognize that we need to take better care of it.

Our impact metrics made our financial metrics more compelling, more inspiring, and more obvious to investors that we were revolutionizing the hotel experience. Our impact metrics helped us stand out, and yours will too if you allow these metrics to be an integral part of your business strategy.

Soon, it will be expected of every business to have clear impact metrics they can track and report. Consumers now demand businesses to lead with their values and positively contribute to the world. If you can show how your business is moving us forward, driving change, and doing good while also doing well, your business will be in a strong position. If you have not thought about impact up until now, look at the United Nations' seventeen sustainable development goals for inspiration. Ask yourself how your business could contribute toward one or more of those goals. What impact could you drive through your business? What could you start tracking in your business that would show your commitment to impact? Before I stepped down as CEO of Under Canvas, we started initiatives toward becoming a zero-waste company, which is an enormous undertaking but was part of our company's ongoing commitment to becoming even more environmentally conscious than we already were.

Knowing Your Data

Knowing these key metrics will change how you build and pitch your business. Understanding how things are valued and the metrics that create value provides insight into how you too could create value. These metrics are keys that can open doors.

In 2017, almost two years after I first went out to try and raise capital and five years after we found product-market fit in Yellowstone, we finally closed our first round of investment, bringing institutional capital into the business. The success of my business was a direct product of everything I had learned from the hundreds of noes I received along the way and the countless awkward conversations with investors. I had come to realize that not only had learning the metrics of my business allowed us to get funded, but it had also helped me build a better, more valuable business. In the end, it was my understanding of my own metrics that made it possible for me to pitch an investable business. These metrics were the building blocks of a valuable business, guiding me on my journey and allowing me to make a successful sales pitch for investment.

At the end of the day, the pitch deck is a sales pitch. Demonstrating to investors that you understand and know your own metrics matters and is the key element in showing that you understand what makes an idea sellable. After reading the revenue page in your deck, your reader should be in no doubt about how your company makes money and what your revenue model looks like. We should understand your unit economics and your financial plan. Above all else, we should understand the story you are telling through your numbers. We should understand where you are going, what you are planning, and why you will be successful.

The great news about understanding these metrics is that you can now work on your business and refine it. If your business does not have great, compelling metrics today, figure out what you could do to adjust and make changes in your business to improve performance. Do you need to grow faster? Do you need to reduce your cost of customer acquisition? Maybe you still need to discover your scalable marketing channel and find ways to increase your customer retention and lifetime value. Having clarity around your cash burn will make you laser-focused on how many more months your business will stay alive unless you put more money in the bank. Don't be afraid of your metrics—allow them to inform and guide you. Use them to prove to the world that you are building a valuable business and that you've got the data to back you up. In business, your metrics are your best friend.

Questions for Reflection

- Does a lack of financial knowledge make you feel inadequate? Don't let yourself be intimidated by big fancy acronyms!
- Do you know what the most important metrics are for your business? Are you tracking those metrics?
- Do you need help calculating any of your metrics? If so, who could help you? A chief financial officer (CFO)-type figure is your ideal helper here.
- How confident are you in communicating your most important metrics and how able are you to speak to your trends?
- Do you have impact metrics that you could start to track? What good is your business attempting to do in the world?

Slide Six of the Pitch Deck: Revenue

In my role as a venture capitalist, I love seeing a basic financial forecast for the next five to seven years on your revenue page. Presenting a basic financial model gives a great snapshot of how you are thinking about your growth over time and allows us to quickly see your projected revenue numbers and EBITDA calculations. In addition, you can then also highlight some key pertinent metrics that are critical to your business. You may find there are other metrics that we've not discussed that indicate the health of your business. You should tell investors all the important data points they should know. You can never really give us too many metrics, and it is important to remember that this slide is the place to tell your business story in numbers.

Traction and Proof of Concept

You don't just declare to the world, 'This is who we are,' and it magically happens. You have to prove it to yourself, to your customers and to your employees.

—Tony Bodoh

"You are not good enough," shouts the voice in my head like a broken record on permanent repeat. This recurring thought has caused me to constantly strive to prove myself. Prove myself worthy. Prove myself capable. Prove my critics wrong. Prove I am good enough. For as far back as I can remember, there has always been something inside of me constantly striving to achieve. A compulsion to be the best. To perform, deliver, and compete. Even as a young child, I pushed myself hard, seeking to come first on every occasion. If I could just win, surely I would prove that I was good enough. Winning was never enough to silence that thought, but I pushed harder nonetheless. I'm sure I imagined that if I could drown that thought out under a mass of achievement, it would finally go away. To be clear, it still hasn't.

Obsessive striving has driven me directly into the arms of burnout more times than I would like to admit, causing mental, physical, and emotional crashes. The first and worst time was in my mid-twenties, when I encountered the stark reality that I am not superwoman, not invincible, not without limits, not all-powerful, nor capable of being everyone's or even my own savior. It was a blessing and a curse all at the same time, because I loved being superwoman. This borrowed identity was infinitely more endearing than not being good enough. Being superwoman felt empowering, strong, and almost safe. Yet being superwoman was only half the story. Superwoman also had to reconcile her soft underbelly, her vulnerabilities, emotions, needs, and very real limits alongside that fire within her that causes her to push hard.

I've come to understand that it's not the fire within me that's dangerous; that fire is incredibly powerful and effective. It contains within it the potential to make incredible things happen. Still, it's our lack of awareness, our unconsciousness, that makes us vulnerable to our core instincts, making us limited by them rather than propelled. To be real superwomen, we must harness our instincts, harness our inner wounds, and leverage them to our advantage. We need to transform our thinking from "I'm not good enough," in my case, to "I'm enough as I am." That combination of renewed thinking and harnessed instincts is powerful.

By 2012—the real culmination year for our business when we had set up a tented hotel in Yellowstone—I knew this was our final attempt to make our venture work. After three years in Montana with not much progress to report other than a lot of credit card debt and a failed business in the UK before that, it was "do or die." I especially felt the angst of not just proving to ourselves we could make something work, but proving to our families that we were smart, talented people and not crazy fly-by-nights off on another harebrained scheme. Although nothing was said out loud, I felt that everyone else thought we were crazy. But as Steve Jobs famously said, "Here's to the crazy ones, the misfits, the rebels, the troublemakers, the round pegs in the square holes. The ones who see things differently…they push the human race forward. And while some may see them as the crazy ones, we see genius. Because the people who are crazy enough to think that they can change the world, are the ones who do."[1]

I was crazy with a point to prove, crazy enough to believe we could build a world-class business that could do an enormous amount of good. I'm sure if I had not felt like I had something to prove or did not have a strong desire to achieve, I might have given up before we got our breakthrough. Given up when a storm rolled in, given up when no one seemed interested in funding us. Yet an inner determination and strong drive to succeed likely saved our business. All too often, we listen to the voices in our heads, allowing them to hold us back, stop us in our tracks, and keep us playing small. Yet, our inner wounds can often be harnessed and used to our and others' benefit. We all have core wounds that affect us in one way or another. Most of us can identify with having a recurring phrase of some kind in our heads that seeks to diminish us. No doubt, somewhere way back when, I missed out on feeling unconditionally loved when I needed to hear and feel it most. This left a void that I still attempt to fill by driving myself hard. But this unquenchable thirst to be seen and recognized has also created an enormous drive that has helped me achieve some extraordinary things. Though in the past I have driven myself to the point of burnout and exhaustion, "not feeling good enough" has been fuel, driving me to achieve and excel. It has put a fire in my belly, for which I am thankful because now that I can harness it with self-awareness, I can recognize the inherent dangers of pushing myself constantly, but I can also know I can make big things happen.

You, too, are likely used to having to prove yourself. It is an exhausting but not unfamiliar reality for many women who strive to succeed in a working world where they traditionally have not belonged. In my lifetime, global Western society has shifted from most women staying home to raise children to most women being employed in some capacity. Today, in the United States, the labor force participation rate of women has risen to over 60 percent. However, women still face numerous challenges and barriers: wage disparity, lack of flexible working hours, sexual harassment, discrimination, stereotyping, bias, and limited representation in leadership positions, to name a few. These challenges frequently make us believe that we must armor up, show no weakness, and drive ourselves harder than our male counterparts. Yet I've come to realize that real superwomen are also vulnerable, honest, and not afraid of their weaknesses and imperfections. They can take what is often used against them, including those internal voices, and use them as fuel to prove we have what it takes to build extraordinary businesses.

Proof

Traction, the focus of the next page of the pitch deck, is all about demonstrating proof. Proving that we've got a product people want and that they are prepared to pay for it. Communicating your traction is about demonstrating what you have achieved by showing what is working in your business and proving there is demand for your product or services. You will clearly state:

- Achievements to date,
- Number of customers acquired so far,
- Sales to date,
- Successful sales channels,
- Customer conversion rate, and
- Cost of customer acquisition (CAC).

This page provides your sales and marketing data achieved thus far as demonstrated proof of momentum.

Having traction is the difference between having an idea and having a real functional business where people utilize your services or buy your products. You've leaped, and you are actively doing business. Countless people have good ideas, but if there is no traction—no existing customer base to prove that people will pay for your vision—it's difficult to get investors to buy into the dream. Traction of some kind is critical to demonstrating that your business works, and that people want and need what you are offering. Can you demonstrate that you have a value proposition that people want and are prepared to pay for? Can you outline your traction using some metrics we explored in Chapter 5?

Minimum Viable Product

It is easy to imagine that entrepreneurs at the ideation stage of business development must build out a completely perfected idea to start gaining traction. But this is not the case. I often hear pitches from entrepreneurs that tout huge, fantastical dreams for building something quite complicated that will take a great deal of money to build and even more money to sustain on the path toward profitability. I tell those founders, "You are under no obligation to build your ultimate, end-dream product on day one. You don't need to produce the finished version of what you want to sell immediately." Instead, I ask, "Can you quickly and as cheaply as possible, build a basic version, a minimum version of your idea, to prove that people want it and that it is worth spending money on before you build the all-singing, all-dancing, amazing version?" Without testing your idea, you have no opportunity to get feedback from your customers along the way, and you might end up building something people don't want. Building a minimum viable product (MVP) allows you to test the product and learn from the consumer.

During our first three years in business, we ventured into three initial minimum viable products (MVPs) to evaluate their potential. Our journey began at the Dusek family farm in rural Montana, where our tent product showed promise but lacked the customer base we desired.

The next MVP, our event product, uncovered a niche market with potential for a small-scale business model. It wasn't until we launched Under Canvas as a tented hotel in Yellowstone that we had a viable MVP with a business model that could be scaled. Suddenly, we knew we had discovered a large market for our product. After three years of testing different business models, we had finally created a product that we believed was scalable and that we knew people wanted. We were inundated by an overwhelming number of guests that first summer, even with the unfortunate incident of our tents collapsing in a big thunderstorm! However, that first summer served a necessary purpose. We finally had a business model that had traction.

An MVP shouldn't be thought of as only a basic version of your product but as a viable basic version of your product that significant numbers of consumers have demonstrated they want and are willing to pay for. Your MVP should, therefore, be able to help you determine your actual business model. Our event business and tented hotel businesses were effectively utilizing the same product. Still, the MVP was not proving sufficiently viable in the event business because the business model wasn't scalable. It wasn't until we adapted the business model and created a tented hotel experience that the product became viable, and we finally had a successful MVP. The product did not create a sustainable business model, but adjusting the business model in response to the tests created an MVP. An MVP can be basic in its form, but it also has to prove viable, which is only determined by testing your product with your consumers.

What could or does your MVP look like? Have you experimented with various iterations of your MVP? Does your tech product need to just be a front interface while you manually perform all the functions on the back end? Remember, an MVP just needs to function so you can test it; it doesn't need to be perfect.

One of my early investments was in Koa Academy, an online school for grades 4 through 12 in South Africa. When it launched, it was easy to assume that an expensive learning management system would be necessary for their pilot program. However, without the capital needed for that kind of technology platform, the cofounders, Lauren and Mark Anderson, scaled back their initial offering, launching a curriculum for grades 4 through 9 with a simplified platform that needed a significant amount of manual input on the backend. Arguably, it seemed impossible to launch an online school without a significant investment in its technology platform. But they didn't allow their lack of capital or inability to build their ideal platform to stop them from launching. Instead, they used their MVP to get traction, learn from their learners about what they wanted, and prove that their online school was a model that was wanted and needed in South Africa. They were able to use the information they learned from their MVP to build the next version of their business more efficiently, and they are continuing to learn and grow before investing extensive capital in their tech stack.

Discovering which functionality is superior or important takes time, but it allows us to listen and learn from our customers. What we think will be most critical to our customers or users is often not as crucial as we think.

When we first launched Under Canvas in Yellowstone, we were exceptionally concerned about whether people would be happy to pay to sleep in a tent. We didn't know how much people would be prepared to pay, so we offered a range of tent types with varying prices. Our cheapest options utilized shared bathroom facilities and had camping cots and sleeping bags. Whereas our most expensive tents had private bathroom facilities, a real bed with plush sheets and a duvet, and a wood-burning stove for warmth.

We knew our target audience was the mass-market consumer, not the ultra-luxury, high-net-worth consumer. We imagined our guests as young families with children like our own with average incomes. With that perspective, we searched for the comfort zone of what those customers would pay. We were concerned about the ceiling of what they *could* pay. So, most of our tents in that initial season were the least expensive type that shared a communal bathroom. The more expensive tent type, with its own bathroom inside, cost more to build, so we only had a handful of those in our inventory. Our lack of personal resources had influenced our projection of what we imagined our customers would want.

However, we quickly learned that most people wanted tents with private bathrooms and were prepared to pay more for that feature. If I had gone all in, spending millions of dollars building the low-end tent option, I would have built the opposite of what my market wanted. Having an MVP that we were also ready to accept wasn't our finished version served us well and allowed us to continue to adjust, pivot, adapt, and listen to our consumers.

Too often, entrepreneurs don't bring their dreams to fruition because they think they need millions of dollars to build their vision. But that just isn't true. Yes, that initial version may be less sexy and invariably more work to pull off, as your business might need to be infinitely more manual, but it will get you off the ground and allow you to get some traction proving what does and doesn't work. In the beginning, we could not have afforded to build a wide range of infrastructure and lots of expensive tent units. We had to make do with what we could pull off. But launching, even imperfectly, with an MVP allowed us to prove we were on to something, and that people were prepared to pay to stay in a tent.

Until our first year in Yellowstone, we had convinced very few people to come and stay in one of our tents in the Montana wilderness. After our first Yellowstone season (minus Kevin Costner, unfortunately), we had traction with the idea and could prove that thousands wanted what we had to offer. We demonstrated that we could create a magical experience with hot water, flushing toilets, showers, comfortable beds, towels, and cleaning services. While the idea certainly was not the finished product, we had tapped into a concept that people seemed to love, even though we had only scratched the surface of what was possible. That is all that is necessary with an MVP; show that you have a viable version of your product, and that people will pay for it.

Under Canvas today looks almost unrecognizable from the first version we launched in 2012. Still, it got us on the path to building something big and gave us the traction we needed to build an investable business. How can you shift your mindset to allow yourself the gift of imperfection? As you develop your MVP and collect the various data points that will allow you to prove to potential investors whether your business is a viable investment, give yourself permission to produce or offer something to your customers that can be improved later.

Minimum Quantity of Sales

Once you've got your MVP, you need it to start generating sales or acquiring users so you can demonstrate that people will pay for or use your products or services. To be investable for a seed round of investment, you typically need to demonstrate that you have generated at least $50,000 worth of sales in one year or created a significant online user base to prove that you have a viable idea. You need to demonstrate that you have a product or service that people want and are purchasing.

A *seed round* of investment is typically the first type of institutional investment round where venture capitalists (VCs) consider investing, after your friends, family, and angels have helped you get your business started. Generating $50,000 in sales is a low baseline metric that works even in less developed economies. You can think of that metric as $4,000 a month of recurring revenue or annual payments that total up to $50,000.

If you haven't yet reached that threshold, then you typically need to think about funding yourself through your network to get you off to the races and get you on that track. Remember, as discussed in Chapter 4, having your skin in the game also demonstrates to VCs that you are all in and committed to your idea. Having to come up with the resources to get your idea off the ground increases your impetus to make things work.

While $50,000 could generally be considered the floor for demonstrating traction, the higher your revenue, the greater the traction you will have and potentially even more evidence to prove you are on to something, which creates increased confidence. Remember, VCs generally don't like investing in ideas without traction. Your traction to date proves that you are on to something and that with more capital in your business, you could scale more rapidly, refining and developing your products or services.

Understanding the milestones of what is expected for each fundraising round helps us identify the goalposts and the funding target. That $50,000 potentially gets you to the starting line for funding, but you'll need to demonstrate you've done at least $1 million in revenue before fundraising for your Series A round, the next round of funding after a seed round. Knowing the next milestone is $1 million in revenue should help you consider leveraging any seed round funding to help you reach that milestone. Your existing traction should help you raise capital to demonstrate the required level of traction to make your company investable. Traction hopefully begets traction.

Making Sales Happen

One of the most challenging aspects of growing and scaling a business while demonstrating traction is reaching those elusive revenue thresholds by driving sales. This exceptionally critical revenue generating aspect can be uncomfortable, unfamiliar, and awkward. Unfortunately, driving sales is the fundamental element that drives growth and creates access to funding.

Colombian native Monica Hernandez, CEO and cofounder of MAS Global Consulting, a software engineering consulting firm based in Florida, remembers when she first started her business and her fear of winning new clients. She didn't want to come across as a pushy salesperson and felt she didn't know how to talk about her business with potential clients. Her nerves, however, served as her best asset as she discovered her own strategy, which helped her overcome those fears and unknowns. Upon meeting new potential clients at conferences and events, Monica started asking those connections for insights and advice as she pitched them her services. She would ask them for specific guidance regarding what would make it appealing for someone in their position to do business with her company. Genius! Monica's request for assistance was often received very positively, enabling her to spend more time with her potential customers. She would show up with her questions from the onset, ready to learn from her potential customers, and at the same time, she would subtly be sharing more about her business and building an important relationship. She was there to learn how to communicate more intelligently to the future chief technology officers she would encounter (the usual buyer of her services). Still, she also got an opportunity to position her company firmly in that client's mind, sharing her passions and her company's skills, experience, and values. For Monica, learning precipitated sales and built relationships that genuinely created the opportunity to add value to each other. As she got to know her potential customers, she was able to engage with the problems the client was having and share case studies of what she had done previously to help solve that specific problem, creating value for them. This process allowed Monica to win potential clients' confidence and gain the opportunity to solve those problems for them, time after time.

Monica didn't need to come in with a rote sales script. She simply needed to listen to her customers and provide something they needed. Ultimately, sales are all about providing value to the customer, understanding their needs, and presenting them with solutions to those problems. Monica learned to do her homework when she showed up for meetings with potential clients, so she could be ready with some level of education about their business. This allowed her to ask them increasingly intelligent questions so she could tailor what she shared about her company accordingly. She wanted to position her company as a provider of solutions for the person in front of her, adding value to them and creating a way out of the problem they were facing.

Monica recalled the freedom she felt when she realized that driving sales doesn't have to look one way. She knew it didn't have to be a cold, hard sell. She also realized that learning to adapt and be herself was critical. Women don't need to imitate the selling style we've seen men in sales roles perform; it doesn't have to feel masculine or uncomfortable. We simply need to find the slipper that fits our own feet. Monica's strategy of relationship-building and asking for guidance has helped her client base grow exponentially.

Find your own path that feels suited to your style and personality. Whatever you do, don't shy away from driving sales. A business that thrives will continually grow its sales.

Sales Strategy

A strategy for driving your sales is the next critical component in making those sales happen. Last year, Monica decided to triple the size of her company in the following three years. Everyone in the company, therefore, knew about their plan for "MAS 3×," or three times more in Spanish, Monica's native tongue. Putting real numbers into her growth strategy was the first step so that she and her team could start asking, "What is it going to take to make that happen?" Breaking down your numbers into bite-size chunks allows you to brainstorm how you will generate those numbers and what growth might look like practically. I frequently run a brainstorming exercise with the entrepreneurs I work with, where we bring all of our ideas for driving growth to the table. We then ask ourselves, out of all those ideas, Which initiatives have the most potential to drive the most growth, or which seems the most significant? After debating and contemplating, we look to determine the top three strategic initiatives (ideas) for driving growth so that those become the focus of our energy and efforts throughout the next quarter or year. None of us can do everything at once; we need to break down our big goals into smaller ones to help us execute our plans. When everyone in the company knows our goals and our top initiatives for the quarter ahead, the whole team can start to contemplate how they could contribute towards driving that growth.

One of the biggest hurdles to scaling a business is not having a clear strategy for how you will drive sales. It's not enough to project great numbers into the universe without a clear blueprint of where those numbers will come from. Understanding where your sales have come from so far and where they could come from in the future is part of determining whether something is scalable and creating an actionable plan toward achieving your growth targets.

Marketing Channels

A growth channel is a marketing channel that will work for your business to increase and drive sales. Finding your ideal marketing channel is much like finding a slipstream of fast-moving water that will take you where you want to go in the fastest time possible. Maybe most of your customers come from Facebook marketing, TikTok videos, or Trip Advisor listings. Your channels are how people discover you exist and become users of your products and services. Investors will be looking at whether you've found your slipstream yet—your highly scalable, low-cost growth channel—and if there has been any cohesion around what has driven your sales to date. Today, there are an infinite number of ways to connect with customers. Increasingly, those ways are digital, but your digital presence can take many forms. Your specific target customer will affect which digital channels might be most effective for your business.

In 2020, Anouck Gotlib, cofounder of Belgian Boys, whom we met in Chapter 2, discovered that TikTok might be a leading channel for her brand when an employee asked her, "Have you heard of this new craze for pancake cereal on TikTok?" At the height of the COVID-19 pandemic, one woman's TikTok post about making tiny pancakes with leftover batter in her kitchen went viral. She created tiny pancakes and started eating them in a bowl like cereal. The idea took off, and people started making pancake cereal in their homes, creating the pancake cereal trend on TikTok. The pancake cereal trend on TikTok currently has over 1.7 billion views. This sparked an incredible idea for a company that specialized in Belgian sweet breakfast treats. Could they bring to life an idea born on TikTok and make pancake cereal a real-life commercial product? In partnership with Target, Anouck and her team did just that. She took a viral trend on a social media channel and brought it to life in stores. She connected to a highly popular trend on TikTok and aligned her brand in that space by creating a new commercial product that did not exist on the shelves. Suddenly, Belgian Boys have the eyes of 1.7 billion people on them. Anouck welcomed the opportunity to connect with a young, new audience uniquely and allowed a viral trend to drive product innovation and growth.

Since being active on TikTok, Belgian Boys has driven consistent engagement with their content, which consistently goes viral, with posts garnering views from hundreds of thousands of people. This platform has become their highly scalable, low-cost growth channel, which allows them to connect with their consumers, drive engagement by following and connecting to TikTok trends, and even bring TikTok trends to life.

Finding the channel that will work best for your business will likely take time and money, but finding that channel will help you position your business in your marketplace and create the building blocks needed to grow and scale. Remember in Chapter 2 when I shared that I realized that our events business would be hard to scale, forcing us to look for a different business model? That realization came about because we couldn't find a scalable marketing channel that would help us acquire customers regularly. Our event rental business relied on people being inspired to have their own tented event and those customers picking up the phone to call us. There was very little we could actively do to market that business, apart from pushing out great imagery of beautiful tents into the world to inspire our potential customers. Our lack of a scalable marketing channel indicated that the tented event business would be hard to scale, and that growth would be more haphazard, making growth very difficult to achieve and gain investment for because there was no clear path to drive it.

Being able to actively drive growth becomes a significant characteristic of investable businesses. Discovering the marketing channels that work best for your business as fast as possible is critical to determining sufficient traction and persuading VCs that you could effectively use more capital in your business to help you drive more growth. VCs know that it often requires funding to figure out what marketing strategy will work best for your business, and therefore, using some of your seed funding to help you determine your best sales strategy should be anticipated. However, demonstrating what your current marketing channels look like on your traction page and how they currently perform will be a helpful indicator for both you and your potential investors. Who knows? Maybe a TikTok trend is out there waiting for you!

Conversion Rate

Converting customers from onlookers and observers to actual paying customers is what I often call a volume game. You need to present your product or service to enough people to get some people to buy. How many people are converted by your sales efforts is known as your conversion rate. Your conversion rate indicates how effective your sales and marketing channels are. To drive sales, we must build our marketing strategy, determining how many potential customers we need to reach with our marketing efforts to convert our potential customers into paying customers. For example, you might discover that you have to show your advertising campaigns to five hundred people to get one person to click and buy. Or, in the TikTok analogy, you might need a viral campaign to drive brand awareness and, ultimately, store purchases. Your conversion rate could also be how well your website converts visitors into paying customers. Your conversion rate represents the ratio between how many people you are in front of and how many of them spend money with you. You know there is a problem if you have a lot of eyes on you, but you aren't converting those eyes into actual paying customers.

Ideally, as we get better at determining what sales channels work best, we will see your conversion rate increase over time. Your conversion rate is a metric that helps you see the health of your business. What converts, and what doesn't? What are we wasting money on because it doesn't convert well? How many people need to go to the top of our sales engine to get the results we are trying to achieve?

Much like breaking down our big revenue goals, we can also break down our sales targets to help us figure out mathematically how many calls we need to make, how many ads we need to show, and how many campaigns we need to run. The smarter we can get with this data, the better. Do you know how well you are converting? Could you succinctly say what your conversion rate looks like?

How well you are converting potential customers into real sales indicates where we might have churn (a leak at the bottom of the bucket) and where we have holes down the sides as well. Getting visibility on this data will help you see where the problems are in your business and will help drive sales more efficiently.

How Much Will Your Customer Pay?

The final component of traction demonstrates that your customer will pay for your product or service and how much your customer will pay. For example, suppose you have a product that costs you ten dollars to make, but your customer will only pay ten dollars and fifty cents for it. In that case, you will know that those margins are insufficient unless you have a strategy and a business plan to sell an enormous volume of that product, like Walmart's business model. However, most startups lack the resources or market to compete with giants like Walmart. We, therefore, are typically looking for and need to demonstrate that we have outstanding gross profit margins on our products and services. Ideally, we are shooting for a gross profit margin of 30–50 percent or better. Can I make or deliver a product or a service that costs me less than 50 percent of the customer's price? In other words, if it costs me $50 to make or produce a product, can I sell it for $100? That would give me a 50 percent gross profit margin.

I had no idea what our guests would pay when we first launched Under Canvas in Yellowstone, which is why we offered a variety of price points. But as we quickly discovered the tent types that were most in demand and eliminated the lower-priced tents, we also discovered an appetite for even more expensive tented options than we had originally imagined. Over time, we were able to introduce a larger suite tent that had a lounge area and could sleep up to four people, a stargazing tent that allows you to lie in bed and look out at the stars at night, and family tents that allow multiple tents to be positioned together to allow families to have their own larger private area. The ceiling for what our guests were willing to pay for the experience was much higher than I originally imagined. The appetite and demand for incredible experiences were high. Demand for a product in limited supply can, of course, also help you increase the cost of your product or service. Our customers will often surprise us with what they are willing to pay for our products and services, especially where there is perceived additional added value. Under Canvas has become more than a nice place to sleep at night. Under Canvas is known for creating unique experiences for families, friends, and colleagues to gather, connect, and have unique experiences out in nature. The vision behind the company of creating a unique lifestyle brand means that Under Canvas is more than a tented hotel company.

Confidence

Painting the picture of your traction builds confidence and indicates what you and your business could do in the future. You don't need to have a perfect product or service before gaining traction, but you do need an MVP to help you start driving sales. Driving sales is not a straightforward exercise, but there is much to be learned as your customers start buying from you. Demonstrating initial sales information and sales and marketing trends, along with what you've learned about your preferred channels and data around your price point, will not only provide valuable data to a VC; it will also show you where to work on your business. Just as our initial MVPs showed us how to continue iterating our business further, your traction will show you where you need to pivot, adjust, test, find new solutions, or keep building. Traction proves your business journey and is a steppingstone towards your future growth. Gaining traction is proving to yourself and the world that you are on to something and that you might not be as crazy as others might think!

Questions for Reflection

- What does the critical voice in your head say to you? Can you use your awareness of that voice to not hold you back, but propel you forward instead?
- Are you used to having to prove yourself? How can you leverage this to your advantage?

- Do you have sufficient traction to prove you have customers who want your product or service and are prepared to pay for it? If not, what key steps can you take today to increase your traction?
- Do you feel uncomfortable or awkward with the notion of driving sales? Why? What would it take for you to push through the discomfort and find your unique sales strategy?
- Have you discovered your highly scalable and relatively low-cost growth channel yet? What marketing channel is working best so far for your business?
- How could you continue to improve your performance on that channel?

Slide Seven of the Pitch Deck: Traction

Show us all your most important sales and marketing metrics indicating what you've achieved to date. Tell us how many people are using your services and what revenue you've generated so far. Indicate what marketing channels work best for your business and your pricing. Your conversion rate and acquisition cost may also be helpful indicators of your trajectory so far. You can exclude these metrics if you don't have enough conversion data yet.

The Competition

The biggest risk to your business isn't the competition. It's if you get distracted and influenced by it and dilute your own secret sauce.

—Jamie Kern Lima

When you've spent a long time building something significant that has cost you blood, sweat, and tears, it's natural to want to defend it and protect it from harm or derision. The instinct to preserve and maintain what you have is strong when it has cost you a lot to get where you are now. I distinctly remember the nervousness I felt each time we decided to double down on ourselves and keep taking further risks to grow our business. Whenever we went out on a limb to sign for a new piece of land or do something we'd never done before, we jeopardized what we had already built. I asked myself, "Would this be the risk that sinks us? Is this a bridge too far?" Yet without making those leaps and taking risks to make more happen, we would have been stuck and more likely to get left behind in the wake of our competitors. We could not afford to play it safe. We had to keep building, growing, moving faster, being bigger, and being out front. An offensive strategy became our best strategy to protect what we were building. This is often where we see entrepreneurs make some of their biggest mistakes, frequently causing the very downfalls they were trying to prevent. When we stop taking risks, stop innovating, and stop doing new things and instead start playing it safe or playing defensively, then we fall into dangerous territory. When we act defensively, we will never be able to win new ground, resulting in a struggle to keep the ground we've got. Playing it safe makes us more vulnerable to attack and to losing the ground we have worked hard to gain.

I see this "play it safe" mentality frequently in women, and surprisingly often when women raise capital for the first time. When Melissa (name changed for anonymity) took some initial seed capital to help her fledgling product company grow, she became overwrought with fear. She worried obsessively about running out of cash instead of investing in her growth, building her team, and driving her sales engine. Her fear caused her to hold back on making important decisions and investing capital in the business. Instead, she kept the cash in the bank until, eventually, it was whittled away, and her fear became reality. Without having built the sales engine in her business, her sales dried up, and the cash in the bank ran out. She inadvertently sealed the fate of her business by seeking to preserve what she had rather than building for the future. Because she could see the risks of building her team and not having the cash she needed to continue to pay them long-term, she chose not to build that team. She failed to appreciate that if she didn't build, she would not drive sales and fail to succeed. She looked at the risk instead of the opportunity cost of not doing something. The opportunity cost turned out to be much more costly.

The temptation to protect cash by metaphorically burying it in the ground while avoiding risks and not investing in growth or making smart investments is like signing your own business' death warrant. Playing safe or playing small is never a good strategy. Instead, we need to go on the offensive, play bigger, and not worry about preserving what we have, but instead recognize that we put it all at risk by clinging tightly to what we've got. We must be prepared to take risks to drive growth. "Go big or go home" is a much better defense strategy than "playing it safe."

Go Big or Go Home

When I discovered that someone else was raising money for an idea like Under Canvas, I knew we had to take the next step in growing our business. If we didn't put more capital into our business, we could lose ground to a well-funded competitor and get left in the dust. I was intensely worried about competition—would we lose our customers to this competitor? Would we lose potential land deals because they were also looking for a similar property? Would that business be better than ours and eventually put us out of business? Despite my initial fears, the competition greatly benefited our growth and the growth of the glamping industry overall. Having another competitor in our orbit meant we needed to step up our game, refine our business, position ourselves distinctly in our market, and focus on what would make us defensible—and that would not be playing safe or small. We had to grow faster and stake our claim, leading this new glamping industry. I realized that raising capital was imperative if we wanted to move faster, do more, and define a whole new hospitality category.

One of the distinct advantages that a new competitor coming into our space provided for us was that they helped our industry grow. The more players that exist in a particular arena, the more it helps define that arena as a new industry. Competitors helped put glamping on the map, as the more options people had where they could go glamping, the more people went glamping. This helped underpin the legitimacy of what we were creating. The amount of money spent collectively on advertising the concept of glamping attracted more customers overall, which was especially impactful in a brand-new industry. It takes significant money to build a new industry, as you not only need to build brand awareness for your company but also for an entirely new industry. When we launched Under Canvas, we could not afford to spend money to convince people that glamping was a thing. The competitors coming into our space helped raise awareness for the Under Canvas brand and the whole concept of glamping. Competition was hugely beneficial for our industry and critical in helping us realize we had to grow faster. It significantly shaped my thinking, helping me realize how important it was to keep moving forward. I didn't need to fear competition. Instead, I needed to allow it to fuel our tank to help us grow.

Competition is inevitable, even if you are the first to do something in a new arena. If what you are doing is great, someone else will ultimately want to do it too. Competition places your business in context and forces us to understand how we will differentiate ourselves, stand out, and up to increasing pressures from like-minded businesses. The competitors' page of the pitch deck outlines your competition and distinguishes your business from theirs. It is your opportunity to draw attention to what makes you defensible by answering three important questions:

- Where and how do you fit in your marketplace—how are you positioning your business?
- Who else is already doing what you do—who are your direct or indirect competitors?
- And how well can your business survive an attack and withstand external and internal threats to the company?

These three elements answer the ultimate question that investors want to know: Is your business defensible?

Positioning: How Big Are You Thinking?

How you position yourself in your market is a huge indicator of how big you are thinking. Do you think like a giant or a mouse? Who you compare your business with speaks volumes about how you envision the potential of your business and your ability to disrupt existing industries.

I recently heard a pitch from a founder wanting to start a new taxi service for women, with exclusively women drivers. It was a brilliant, unique idea with potential because she was selling safety and peace of mind for women while utilizing a taxi service. I don't know about you, but I can't imagine I'm the only woman in the world to ever worry about getting murdered or taken into a dark alley and raped when you get into a taxi. Her concept sounded fabulous. But her positioning did not. She positioned herself in the marketplace by comparing herself to the local taxi services. Although she rightly compared her idea against direct competitors, she also indicated that she was thinking too localized. Her positioning was too small. The type of positioning an investor wants to see should potentially disrupt an entire industry.

This taxi entrepreneur could have changed her positioning by saying, "I'm building a whole new brand of global taxis *for* women *by* women, and I will disrupt Uber." Or "I will be the new Uber for women." Therefore, she could have listed the competitors of Uber, Lyft, or national taxi firms. A simple reframing would have suggested that she intended to take a slice of a multi-billion-dollar worldwide industry.

I passed on the investment because I believed she wasn't thinking about a large enough business model. She was thinking about building a local taxi company in one city, and for a venture capital firm, that is not an investible business. Investors want to see your conviction that you are the future and that you are positioning yourself to uniquely compete in big industries that are ready to be unraveled. Who you compare yourself with is critical to this page of the deck.

Competitive Advantage: How Are You Different?

Once you've determined the right companies to compare yourself against, you must distinguish your business from those competitors. You want to confirm what separates you and why your competitors cannot put you out of business. In other words, what makes you different and defensible against direct and indirect competition? Directly, could someone else set up shop doing exactly what you do, focus on the same target audience or customer as you, and steal your market share? If someone else had much more money to replicate your business, could they wipe you out?

Similarly, could someone do something comparable to what you do and inadvertently or indirectly divert customers from your product or service? Could innovative technology disrupt your business and render it obsolete? How easy would it be for your company to become irrelevant and outdated? What separates you from everyone else? What insulates you? What do you have that can't be easily replicated? What magic formula, secret sauce, or intellectual property (IP) do you have that makes it difficult for someone else to do what you do, how you do it? Do you have anything that is proprietary to the company or that can be patented or trademarked that is essential to doing business the way you do it? Investors are looking for specific things within the business that set your business apart and that give you a competitive edge.

In addition to your unique intellectual property, building a unique brand identity is crucial to creating an iconic, recognizable, repeatable, and, therefore, defensible and valuable business. A strong brand sets out a clear identity and company values, which often communicate that there is more to a company than what it produces or sells. Strong brands connect us to something beyond just a product or service; they make us believe there is something special or unique about connecting with that company. For example, if you want to "Just do it!" you wear Nike. If you want a Big Mac, you look for the golden arches of McDonald's. Coca-Cola makes America's "best-selling soft drink." Branding potentially differentiates them from other hamburger restaurants, soft drink manufacturers, or sneaker companies. Building a strong brand is like building a moat around your company—creating an identity that is hard to replicate, even if your product or service is not that original. Remember, value is created by being unique and different from the original.

At Under Canvas, we recognized that although people have been pitching tents and experiencing safaris since the dawn of humanity, there was an opportunity to revolutionize the concept. We didn't invent the safari experience; we took it, reimagined it, and created something entirely new. We transformed the luxury tent experience into a uniquely branded adventure by reinventing it. While you may be in a competitive market, it's crucial to differentiate from the company down the road. Your unique vision, product, or system has the potential to exponentially increase your ability to produce or sell. A strong consumer brand can create identity and loyalty in a crowded market. How a company is perceived because of its brand can impact its price, speed of adoption, and acceptance of a new business. Poor branding or a lack of company identity can mean the consumer does not connect with a product or service and, therefore, does not purchase or repurchase it. How you present yourself to the world matters.

Similarly, a well-differentiated niche can drive significant value. One company I have invested in is a recruitment company. Recruitment companies are two a penny—nothing new there. But this company has a unique angle. They're developing artificial intelligence (AI) software that will revolutionize the process and the speed of recruitment. Their AI will dramatically diminish the time it takes to recruit someone by analyzing the data to find the perfect candidate for a specific role. They plan to scale their business by selling their AI tool to other companies worldwide, enabling them to build an infinitely bigger revenue stream from the AI software than they ever would from being recruiters. We invested in them because of their AI component—their intellectual property. They are doing something unique that no one has fully nailed—using AI to change the recruitment process. That tool sets them apart and makes them unique.

Having something proprietary, however, doesn't necessarily mean you must have revolutionary technology. For Sherry Deutschmann, former chief executive officer (CEO) and founder of Letter Logic, her secret sauce was her company culture. Her company created extraordinary value because it valued the employees first. The employee-first-driven culture of Letter Logic became Sherry's revenue strategy because she always communicated to her potential new clients that her company was the most expensive out of all of her competitors. She explained her unique differentiator by communicating how heavily she invested in her employees. By demonstrating that her employees were engaged, committed, and responsive because they were well rewarded and shared in the company's profits.

She could position her business to potential clients as far above the rest, even though her service was more expensive than anyone else's. Her secret sauce was investing in her people, who would in turn offer outstanding service and do an excellent job, which built incredible trust and commitment from her customer base, who were prepared to pay top dollar for her services. Letter Logic became the best at what they did—providing a great customer experience for their clients who used Letter Logic to provide invoicing services for medical facilities nationwide. Sherry beat her competitors not by being cheaper but by being better. Sherry's employee-first approach saw her grow the business to more than forty million dollars in revenue and a lucrative exit when she sold the business. Sherry's competitive advantage was selling a service driven by an employee-first approach.

Another way to differentiate your business is to consider what would make you iconic. Under Canvas's unique selling point was our tent design—our most distinctive intellectual property. After our first season in Yellowstone, we understood that an iconic look could help us multiply our business many times. Our tents, designed by my husband Jake and his team, were unique, giving our company a unique look and feel. They became a highly sought-after product by our customers, which in turn caused a great dilemma and internal challenge.

Even after we created Under Canvas in Yellowstone, we continued to field calls to sell our tents. We realized that if we sold our unique tents, anyone could have purchased them and established themselves as our competitors. We decided not to sell our tents because it was the most unique element of our concept. They could not be purchased anywhere, and there was nothing like them on the market. It was an enormously difficult decision because we desperately needed the revenue stream. Staring us in the face, the obvious route was to say "yes" to customers who wanted to purchase hundreds of tents. Selling in bulk would have generated noteworthy, needed revenue. But it also would have set other people up to compete with us directly. Bulk buyers wanted to use our tents to do exactly what we did—they wanted to open a camp and create an experience on their piece of land. Had we sold to such buyers, we would certainly not have been able to build an iconic, distinctive brand that had a clear visual brand identity that was difficult to replicate.

In addition to iconic tents, the way we operated Under Canvas also became a distinct competitive advantage. In our early Yellowstone days, we made a crazy decision, which turned out to be a brilliant choice. We decided not to have Wi-Fi at all our camps, which was potentially risky for a hotel. Given that our mission was to connect people to the outdoors and to each other, we didn't want to connect them to more technology. We knew that our ethos and mission had to impact how we did business, and that decision became part of our competitive advantage.

Most of our guests chose to stay with us mainly to disconnect from technology and to connect outdoors with the people they loved. We consciously decided to differentiate ourselves by saying, "This is who we are. We are not the place to stay if you need a place to work while you travel." That type of distinguishing choice created value, making us more distinguishable from our competitors and our mission more difficult to replicate. It was ultimately more valuable as we carved out our brand distinctions and became known by the consumer.

Iconic designs and value-based distinctions cemented the defensibility of the business. To keep our outdoorsy brand and family-centered culture intact, we had to repeatedly push aside outside pressures to add Wi-Fi. We also had to resist the urge to sell our tents, which would have undermined our product but yielded short-term cash flow. At various inflection points, whenever we needed or were worried about cash flow, we questioned those decisions. I'd love to say my resolve kept us on track, but Jake's clarity very often kept us firmly on this path.

In every entrepreneur's journey, a time comes to decide what is important to protect, what is truly proprietary, and what needs to be carefully guarded or sacrificed for instant revenue. These are tough decisions, especially for the entrepreneur struggling with the day-to-day grind of paying the bills and who may not have a "Jake" to help lift her head from the daily running of the business to focus on the future. When those days come—and they will come—make a conscious decision to take a step away from managing the daily operations and look at your business from above. You must learn to work *on* your business, not just *in* your business. Every problem has multiple sides; therefore, you must look at it uniquely. Dig deep enough to consider what other solutions I have to solve my problem. Maybe I need another interest-free credit card. Maybe I could get a bank loan. Maybe I've got some friends or family who might help. Maybe there's something else that I could do to drive revenue. Maybe I should raise capital. Whatever you do, don't sacrifice what is iconic and special about your business today simply to drive instant revenue.

Once I began thinking about the bigger picture and the long-term, I realized that we could take advanced bookings at our camp to help solve our cash flow issues. When we closed our Yellowstone camp at the end of the first season, we made it possible for customers to book for the next year, and to my surprise, we confirmed bookings with one hundred percent payment for the year ahead in remarkable numbers, which was and continues to be unprecedented in the travel industry. No hotel does that. But we had established an experience in such high demand that people booked and paid one hundred percent for their next stay with us up to an entire year away. Those resources provided significant relief. It did not solve all our problems, but it was one of the important ways we managed the business's cash flow. Of course, there were some risks: people could cancel, and we would have to refund their booking, more than likely having to return cash we had already spent. But we agreed that it was unlikely (other than in a global pandemic) that all our locations would be closed and unable to serve our guests and that all of our guests would want their money back. All choices have risks, returns, challenges, upsides, and downsides. But we measured the risk, and we deemed this risk to be much lower than if we had sold our tents and allowed other businesses to compete with us using our own products. Even in 2020, when this risk of massive refunds materialized, it was not an insurmountable problem for the company. Many of our guests kindly delayed their stay with us until it was safe to travel again—which meant they were rewarded with first choice of rooms and dates and no price increases when Under Canvas did reopen, and in turn, they significantly helped our cash flow.

The decision not to sell our tents was the right one. Despite Jake's early clarity on this issue, it was not until much later that we realized how meaningful this decision had been. Our ability to create enormous value in our company was largely because we not only stood out from the crowd and protected what we offered but also developed a strong national brand with an iconic look. Under Canvas continues to be unique and extremely defensible because of our distinctive tent design and mission-led decisions. The uniqueness of our brand allowed the business to function like the golden arches of McDonald's. The product you love with Under Canvas is the same experience wherever you stay across the country. Only the geography and activities change.

The easier it is for someone to set up shop doing exactly what you do, the less value you create and the less valuable you will be. It is important to think early on: what hurdles can you put in place to make it difficult for people to jump through to copy you? What are the barriers to penetrating your business? Are there enough hurdles? Can you develop your systems, efficiency, intellectual property, and brand recognition sufficiently to differentiate and separate yourself from existing and potential new competitors? Build as many moats around your castle as possible so that you stand out and stand up against the competition.

Surviving Disruption

Investors talk a lot about *disruption* in the venture capital arena, often without a clear definition. Disruption is a significant change or interruption in a particular industry, market, or system that changes how things are done. Disruptions often result in the displacement of existing players, products, or services and the emergence of new and innovative solutions. Various factors, such as technological advancements, regulatory shifts, market demand, or changes in consumer behavior can drive disruptive changes. Clayton Christensen popularized disruptive innovation in his book *The Innovator's Dilemma.*[1] This statement describes how new technologies often disrupt established markets and create new ones. Uber is a good example of this, as it disrupted the global taxi industry as we know it. Suddenly, anyone, anywhere, could become a taxi driver, using their own car to provide a ride to anyone using the app. However, even disrupters can be disrupted, as the previous example of the female taxi company "by women, for women" shows us. There is always room for further disruption. That is why it is critical to demonstrate what industry or market you intend to disrupt and that you will continue to disrupt your own business and evolve and advance rather than wait for a competitor to disrupt you.

It is always much better to disrupt yourself before someone else does it. Don't wait to improve your systems, processes, and products until a competitor comes along, forcing you to be better. Constantly ask yourself, "How do I streamline my business? How do I make it more efficient? How can I improve our product?" I frequently get entrepreneurs to ask, "If we were starting from scratch and had a blank check to compete with what we are already doing, how would we build the business? What would we do differently?" That process forces us to consider what we would stop or start doing. What would we not do? What would we change?

Too often, we get stuck with an outdated business model—one that helped us start the business, but will not help the company continue to grow. Blockbuster must be the most famous example of this. The Netflix founders tell the story of their early days as a mail-order DVD service with a small streaming component. They approached Blockbuster in 2000 to buy them for fifty million dollars, thinking that Blockbuster would want to expand the business they were already in by moving into rentals by mail and then into streaming. Since Netflix was almost entirely out of cash and desperate to keep their fledgling business alive, they pitched the $6 billion DVD giant for funding. Blockbuster dismissed the Netflix founders out of hand. Blockbuster turned them down, failing to see that innovation was essential for survival and that their business model was about to become defunct. Within a few short years, Blockbuster was ruined by that tiny competitor who had been almost out of cash. Blockbuster filed for bankruptcy in 2010. Can you imagine going from being worth $6 billion to declaring bankruptcy? Epic fail. They failed to continue to innovate and allowed themselves and their business model to be disrupted. They failed to imagine a different future, failed to take advantage of new technology, and ended up getting left in the dust by a smaller, nimbler, and innovative company. They played it safe, seeking to maintain what they had instead of making big bets on further innovation and new business models.

Companies have the potential to be disruptive and move the world forward. They change the way we do things, and they change how we do things. They bring the future into our present-day realities. However, every company must either disrupt or be disrupted to withstand becoming obsolete. Ideally, we are the ones disrupting and continuing to disrupt ourselves. Can you succinctly communicate which industry or market you are disrupting? Are you continuing to think about how you disrupt yourself to make bold changes, recognizing that if you don't do it, someone else will do exactly what you could have and should have done?

Investors are looking for people who will disrupt the status quo and build businesses of significant scale that can stand up to some of the biggest external threats of our time.

Surviving Macro Threats

External macro threats like recessions, capital market collapses, and pandemics are some of the most devastating threats because they are beyond our capacity to predict or control. Given the world's recent experience with COVID-19, we know all too well how a global pandemic can disrupt business, render some businesses obsolete, and make others temporarily unable to trade. Every time an investor considers a business for potential investment, they ask themselves, what threats are likely to impact this business and how likely it is to stand up to potential macro threats? Therefore, it's worth taking the time to do that same analysis yourself. Look at your business through the eyes of an investor and ask yourself: Where is my business most vulnerable? What are my biggest risks in the business, and what could I do to strengthen the business against big threats? How do capital markets affect your business? Even just thinking through a downturn, a supply chain crisis, or some other macro threat will help you think about if there is anything else you can do to insulate your business more. Thinking about macro threats also allows you to think through your potential responses and demonstrate confidence in being prepared and able to handle them.

The pandemic broke at the very start of our journey into investing in women-led businesses in Africa. Jake and I analyzed all the companies we were considering for investment, reflecting on whether each business could capitalize on the crisis or be potentially harmed or destroyed. We considered the business's relevancy in the new world we were entering. Could each business thrive through school and office closures and limited travel? Would the pandemic render the services essential or obsolete? Thankfully, all the businesses we invested in weathered the pandemic storm, and many encountered opportunities that spurred growth faster than they had originally planned. Many investors paused their activities in 2020 and cautiously waited to see how the world would shake out. We did not. While we passed on some businesses that were in our pipeline because they had not demonstrated that they could survive the macro threat to the world, we made big bets on other more resilient and big-thinking founders who demonstrated they could weather the global storm. We doubled down on our thesis to invest in women and looked for resilient businesses that could grow during a crisis.

Very few of us were ready for a pandemic in 2020. But if you think through all the levels and ways in which a threat could come, you will build critical resilience in your business. Working *on* the business forces you to think strategically about needle-moving efforts that will transform your business, enabling it to respond to some of the toughest market challenges. Companies built through tough economic or social times will often have the marks of robust, well-managed businesses that are able to go the distance.

When we launched Under Canvas Yellowstone back in 2012, we had no idea that we were, in effect, building a recession and pandemic-proof business. Having started the business originally during a recession and later enduring a pandemic, we had little idea that our tented hotel experience would be extraordinarily resilient to macro threats. Having a local travel product that was accessible to our domestic consumers, enabling them to have unique outdoor travel experiences in nature and in a socially distanced way turned out to be a very robust business model. During the pandemic, the demand for nights at an Under Canvas property became unprecedented. I often thought getting tickets for the Super Bowl would be easier than booking a night at Under Canvas!

Looking at your business model and examining what makes it robust can help you build a strong, defensible business.

Standing Strong

Every investor I have ever pitched has always wanted to understand how defensible my business was. After all, no one wants to put money into something that could be wiped out tomorrow by an external threat or competitor. There needs to be some rigor and long-term viability to your business—you need to prove that a big thunderstorm will not easily blow it over! The more proprietary elements your business has, such as intellectual property or competitive advantages, the better. The more you can demonstrate your company is robust and able to withstand challenges and potential micro and macro threats, the more likely you are to attract others to join you on your journey. This is especially true if you've painted a picture that you are disrupting an industry and building something with huge potential, and compared yourself with the companies you want to emulate, who you think you can be, or who are doing elements of the work you intend to do. Do not place yourself in a small box. Dream big and demonstrate why your company will be standing years from now, disrupting long after others have fallen by the wayside. We need to be women who not only take on the tough challenges and the problems of our day, but are not afraid to take on the big boys currently playing in our arenas. We must not be tempted to play it safe or play small; we've got to think bigger than we have ever imagined before and be brave enough to imagine that we could build something strong enough and big enough to disrupt industry leaders. Know what it looks like to defend your territory and be determined to keep taking new territory. We can build defensible businesses that transform our communities, cities, and nations. The key is to think big and be prepared for the inevitable threats that will head in our direction by playing offensively, not defensively, trying to protect and save what we have.

Questions for Reflection

- In what ways are you currently playing it safe? Do you need to worry less about losing what you've got to build something big? How could counting your opportunity costs help you?
- How are you positioning your business? Are you thinking about placing your business alongside some giant-sized competitors?

- Are you thinking big enough to compete with some of the biggest players? If not, why not?
- What industry are you attempting to disrupt?
- What are your competitive advantages? What do you have that's propriety, difficult to replicate, or iconic?
- In what ways do you need to increase the moat around your business?
- What could you do to insulate yourself better from macro threats?
- What do you believe is the greatest threat to your business today?
- On a scale of one through ten, how defensible do you believe your business is today? If you didn't score a ten, what is in the gap, and how could you close that gap?

Slide Eight of the Pitch Deck: Competition

This page is perfect for a table. In the left-hand column, list your business alongside the competitors you believe are the right competitors to compare yourself against. Then, across the top of the table, outline all the distinct characteristics that your business demonstrates. Using those qualities you've outlined, demonstrate which of your competitors has those attributes by adding a simple check mark in a box. Your company should be able to check all the boxes and your competitors only some. This is how you can demonstrate your competitive edge and position yourself in the market by virtue of the caliber of the competitors you have chosen to stack yourself against.

8

Teams for Tomorrow

If you want to go fast, go alone. If you want to go far, go together.

—African Proverb

Creating tented camps in wilderness areas outside National Parks came with inherent dangers and challenges. From extreme weather and unseasonal snowstorms to encounters with diverse wildlife, we faced numerous hurdles. But the challenges of managing and training our staff were often the greatest.

When we first set up camp in Yellowstone, we were inherently worried about the risk that bears potentially posed to our guests. Bison and bears frequently roamed around in the larger area, and we naturally wanted to ensure our guests were safe. So, we instigated a strict no-food policy in the tents so as not to lure bears to the area, and we provided a can of bear spray in each tent in case of a bear emergency. Staff would inform the guests when they checked in how to use the bear spray in case of a real bear emergency. The instructions seemed clear (to me, at least), so I thought we had a great strategy until two members of our team tried to test out the bear spray, inside a tent, no less, managing to spray themselves and the tent with bear spray. Bear spray is pretty gnarly and as potent if not more so than pepper spray! It stings your eyes, throat, and lungs and stains anything it comes into contact with. It is designed to be an emergency defense when encountering a bear. I couldn't believe it when our employees sprayed themselves and the tent!

In our second year, I thought we'd be smarter. This time, we'd put the bear spray in a clear plastic bag attached to the bed's footboard with a poison warning sticker reminding everyone this is toxic, potent stuff, and you only want to use it in an emergency. However, our staff training that year still failed to be sufficient, because we still managed to have guests who ripped open the bags and sprayed their whole family, including their children, with bear spray, thinking it was like insect repellent but for bears! What a disaster!

In our third year, Jake and I decided to take a different approach. Our managers should be the ones responsible for the bear spray. We removed the bear spray from each tent and placed emergency boxes around the camp for a senior staff member to access in a bear emergency easily and quickly. With the bear spray put away and out of mind, surely we would finally get a year without a bear spray incident. It seemed like we had finally got it right. That was until I got a phone call. "Sarah, I just wanted to let you know that there has been an incident at camp. Our general manager has managed to spray a whole family with bear spray." Me: "Wait, what?! Did you just say the general manager sprayed a family with bear spray?!" Apparently, for some unknown reason, he had gone against protocol and policy and decided to demonstrate how to use the bear spray. Not intending to activate the canister, he inadvertently released the toxic gas into the air, and the spray wafted over the guests. That was his last day working for us and that was the last season we even kept bear spray at our camps. We finally concluded that the risk of the bear spray was much more problematic than bears ever were and that however sufficient we thought our staff training and procedures were, they needed to be infinitely more robust!

People will always surprise us with the crazy things they will do. Every time I think I've seen it all, something unexpected happens. That's why navigating the people side of any business can be one of the hardest things to get right. Building strong teams of people who embody your values, ethics, and ways of being is a hard task, but it is one of the most critical challenges for any founder or chief executive officer (CEO).

People: Your Best Asset

Over time, I've realized that any company's two most valuable assets are cash and people talent. Conversely, the lack of these two assets can be the most crippling factor in any business. These two resources have more impact on a company's future than any other factors. As the founder or CEO, it is, therefore, my most important responsibility to bring not only cash into the business, but also the right people. Ideally, those people won't be spraying your customers with bear spray! It requires bravery and determination to ensure I have both cash in the business and the right people in place to achieve our goals and build the organization I can imagine. It is, after all, people who execute a vision and make things happen. People are the foundation upon whom almost every business is built.

Monica Hernandez, founder and CEO of MAS Global Consulting, whom we met in Chapter 6, reflected on the one thing she would do sooner if she could return and give herself some advice. "I would start building a high-caliber team around me as quickly as possible. I would bring in experts who could bring new ideas, perspectives, and expertise. I would stop thinking I had to do it alone and start leveraging other talent to multiply my talent." I can relate to this, as I understand the allure of wanting to do everything myself, especially when others don't seem as competent, or it's hard to find the talent you need. It's tempting to want to be the expert in every field and to feel like everything depends on me. But as a founder, I need to remember that it's not my job to be the smartest person in the room. Instead, I need the smartest people in the room to help me build what I envision. I need to build a talented team of people around me who become instrumental in helping grow my business. I need to bring in the skills and capabilities I don't possess and build a winning team to navigate each leg of the journey.

Who and How?

One of the questions I always hear from early-stage entrepreneurs now on hiring is, "How do I know who I need when? How should I think about hiring when cash is exceptionally tight?" It is easy to assume that we can't invest in hiring top talent if we don't have surplus cash. But this is not true. By contrast, if we don't have talented people on board, we are unlikely to significantly grow the business and increase our revenue. I couldn't afford not to hire the top talent the business needed, and you can't either.

Too often, women wait to hire, not seeing how essential it is to surround ourselves with talented people. Women get stuck in scarcity mindsets that keep them thinking that resources are scarce rather than getting creative with how to make those resources go a long way. Thinking there is not enough of anything—people, resources, and cash—certainly means there won't be enough. Finding creative strategies to build your team means you will likely create the resources you are looking for.

Instead of waiting and not hiring or being stuck in the mindset that we should just do everything ourselves, we need to get creative and strategic about who to hire and when. Remember when we first hired Doug? Doug was our first big hire after our first season in Yellowstone. He came on board as our chief operating officer and would take on the oversight of operating our camps. We had no resources to fund his salary; we instead worked out a deal to share revenue with him so he could be renumerated. We got creative to bring on board the talent we needed. Subsequently, we hired numerous people who joined us at a lower salary than they were making elsewhere in exchange for some equity in our company and a better work-life balance.

Being a mission-led company also had its benefits in this regard. Creating a pool of stock designated for employees also allowed us to incentivize talented people to come and join us, and was a great way to offset some of the initial up-front salary cost. Offering company stock can be a real incentive for someone thinking about long-term gain. Similarly, levering fractional talent is a way to leverage expertise that you can't afford outright. For example, I now often advise early-stage founders to utilize the services of a part-time chief financial officer (CFO). In the early stages of a business's life, you are unlikely to be able to afford or need a full-time CFO. However, leveraging the expertise of someone who can help you understand your numbers, prepare financial management reports, and help you get better visibility on what's going on in your business can add huge value to your business without adding a huge cost. If I had brought a fractional CFO into our business sooner, my financials would have been in much better shape, and we most likely would have secured a better valuation for our company during our early fundraising days. The fact that our financials were a mess didn't help us present well to investors.

When I consider who to hire next, the most important factor for me is determining who will provide the greatest return on investment (ROI). In simple terms, I look for someone who can bring the most value, significantly impact the business, and potentially pay for themselves through their contributions. While it's common to associate this approach with salespeople, it's crucial to remember that individuals can create ROI in almost any role. Doug is a great example of this. He was an incredible ROI for our organization as he optimized our operations and significantly improved our efficiencies. But perhaps most importantly, he freed up my time to focus on strategic initiatives that propelled our business forward. Because Doug could focus on the business's day-to-day operations, I could stay focused on our big picture. A clear understanding of what I wanted to achieve made it easier to identify the roles I needed to fill to help me realize those objectives. This is half the battle. The other half is finding the right individuals to fill those roles who will align with our vision's ethos and will ensure a strong team culture that can deliver results.

Culture Fit

In the early days of Under Canvas, we consciously decided to hire people who were passionate about the outdoors. We believed that people who loved where they were and who wanted to recreate themselves in nature would potentially be a great fit for what we were trying to create. We believed that if our employees were passionate about getting outside and loved travel, they would love their jobs and advocate for what we were building. These characteristics became the core of our culture fit, but we uncovered additional characteristics that made people a great fit for our company over time. Years later when I was leading a group of female entrepreneurs on a retreat at one of our camps one of the women took me aside and asked me; "I've stayed at several of your camps now and every location has the same great vibe among your amazing attentive staff. How have you been able to do that?" The answer was simple: We hired for our culture fit. Of course, in the early days, we didn't always get this right; we made many hiring mistakes, but our miss-hires also helped us figure out who our people really were. Over time, the kind of people we were looking for became much clearer, and we understood the values we needed people to have. For example, we realized people with high autonomy and a large quantity of common sense were really important in our business.

Culture fit is figuring out what the consistent attributes of your people are. What do they love and like? How do they behave? What do they value? What are the set of behaviors that define the way you want your people to exist together? Hiring for culture fit isn't hiring one specific personality type, but rather developing a clear understanding of how you want people to behave in your company.

Developing a company culture takes time and leadership, as it doesn't happen automatically, or overnight. We started with a foundational love of the outdoors and travel, knowing that we needed passionate people who would be OK working in the sun, rain, snow, and wind. Eventually, we crafted our "rock star" list, which is comprised of a granular look at what all-star players look like. This became my list of qualities and behaviors that define the characteristics of a person that would make them a rock star or an all-star player in my eyes. Here are a few of the characteristics that made it onto my rock star list:

- Operates independently without much supervision and is a self-starter. No one needs to monitor or check on you constantly.
- Brings solutions and doesn't just point problems out for someone else to fix. Solution finders.
- Cares and is passionate about their work and what they are doing. They are emotionally and mentally connected.
- Asks lots of questions in order to learn fast.
- Always assumes the best in others, not the worst.
- Communicates politely. Not rude or abrupt.
- Treats every client, partner, and customer well, demonstrating that we value them deeply even if they do not behave well toward us.
- Doesn't point the finger or blame others. Takes responsibility and owns it.
- Goes above and beyond the call of duty.
- Empowers and supports others, and never thinks or says, "That's not my job."

These are just some of my examples; I probably had twenty more characteristics on my list. This list can be as long as you like, but it should extensively describe behaviors, ways of being, and actions that demonstrate what makes someone a great fit for your company. A behavior should always have an action or actions associated with it. The more actual behaviors are on this list, the easier it is for people to act in those ways. If, for example, you say a rock star is honest, it might be better to define it further by saying, "A rock star is someone who acts the same even when no one is looking. They are honest and trustworthy whether someone is watching or not."

These rock star characteristics were our guideposts in searching for the right people, beyond whether they had the necessary experience or expertise we were seeking. These soft skills or sets of expectations created a much more nuanced approach to hiring and creating the kind of team we were attempting to build. By defining these behaviors, our existing team members could quickly discern if someone was a good fit. It's much easier to spot someone who doesn't fit your culture when you've created an environment where rock stars know what other rock stars look like. Teammates can call each other out if someone is not behaving according to the company's values, as it's easier to say aloud, "Hey, that's not how we communicate or act around here." Other people hiring in your company can also ensure that everyone brings people into your company who all fit the same rock star profile.

Clearly outlining and defining our sense of culture as defined by our values created a strong sense of team, which meant that people felt a sense of belonging and camaraderie within the company. Beyond being a fun place to work, there became a strong sense of being on a mission together, which informed everything we did and why we were doing what we were doing. Our people became connected to the fundamental drivers of why our business existed and they were invested in creating a purposeful, impactful company that thought bigger than simply driving shareholder wealth.

What does a rock star look like to you? What values and behaviors do rock stars exhibit in your eyes? Answering this question will help you unpack your company culture, which may or may not have been verbalized yet. Your answers will also help you build a strong performing team, filled with talented people that exude the company's way of being, which will build a brand that inspires trust, interest, and loyalty from your customers.

What Does Success Look Like?

In addition to defining cultural fit, defining success for each role in your business is similarly important. When people have a clear idea of what is expected of them and what success looks like, they have a greater chance of succeeding in their roles. I often expected people to be mind readers, thinking they should just know what was expected of them. But if we never clearly verbalize our expectations, we inadvertently set people up to fail. By defining success in a specific role, you define clear outcomes for people to drive toward and make happen. Remember, executing your vision is what you are trying to get your team to deliver on. Have you communicated clear goals to your team members? Does everyone know what success looks like in their role? Does everyone in your company have clarity on what your company goals are for the year and the quarter? Do they know what success looks like for them in their role this quarter? Do they know what is required of them and how to succeed?

Communicating expectations helps people execute the most important initiatives and makes it easier to hold people accountable. Verbalizing expectations also allowed me to assess whether I was being realistic. Is what I was expecting humanly possible? Or was I expecting people to pull off mission impossible? I'm afraid to admit that I often asked too much of our people, piling too much pressure on them and attempting to pull off too much in too little time. Sometimes, I needed people to say, "That's pushing people too far." Asking for input on whether your request is reasonable is always a good idea. Ask yourself, "Does my request feel realistic for the experience and pay scale I expect for this role? Is it asking too much? Should someone with a certain set of skills and experience be able to pull it off?" Then, ask others for their take. It was so easy to be blinded by my desire to achieve goals that I became unrealistic and out of touch.

One of the biggest mistakes I see in early-stage entrepreneurs is their attempt to hire one person to plug too many holes. I frequently see job descriptions that combine too many tasks, making it hard for someone to thrive. We set our expectations too high and try to hire one person to take everything off our plates. The reality is that each person you hire can fill a very niche role. Every time Jake or I hired someone in the early days, we expected them to take multiple things off our plates and often take ownership of tasks and responsibilities that were unrelated to each other. We often made the mistake of trying to hire one person to do what was, in effect, ten to twelve people's jobs. We had to learn to break down our workload into distinct roles to enable each new hire to fully focus on a specific niche. We could not, for example, hire one person to do sales and marketing, bookkeeping, customer service, and supply chain management. We had to create specific roles for specific functions and not be overly optimistic about the challenges someone could take on.

We set people up for success when we get realistic about what each role looks like and when we are clear about what success looks like in that role. If people understand success, they can be successful team members. Outlining what success looks like also makes it much easier to communicate when someone is not successful in their role, as you have a benchmark to compare to when expectations are not being met or when expectations have evolved. Remember, roles do evolve, and who and what you need at any given moment will be determined by the leg of the journey that you are on.

Tough Decisions

Five years into our adventure building Under Canvas, the business had grown enormously, with four locations in multiple states. We had gone from just seven people running around like crazy that first summer in Yellowstone to well over one hundred people, including seasonal team members, working at four Under Canvas locations. Doug, our chief operating officer, had done a great job at putting much-needed systems in place, carrying the weight of hiring staff, and helping us operate like a professional hotel company. However, I now knew we were entering our next growth phase, and we needed to shift from thinking and acting like a small, seasonal business to thinking and acting like a well-known, professional, trusted brand. I wanted us to become the "Marriott" of the outdoor hospitality space, and I, therefore, knew we needed to move faster, professionalize the business further, and build a clear brand identity and an exceptionally strong company culture. At the time, we were a scrappy young startup with employees who occasionally sprayed guests with bear spray! I knew if we were going to one day become a one-hundred-million-dollar business, I needed different levels of experience and expertise around me. I needed to build out our executive team with people who had potentially already been where we were going and who could bring their talent to the table to help us get there. The adage "what got you here won't necessarily get you there" seemed true, because I needed people with different levels of expertise and experience around me to help me take our business to the next level. This meant I needed to make the tough decision to say goodbye to some of our original teammates and leaders.

This was, without question, one of the hardest decisions I had made in the business so far, and it was both professionally and personally painful. Making tough decisions, like letting someone go to build the kind of team that could go on the next leg of our journey, was going to be one of the leadership tests that would determine whether I could build a great company. Being able to think big picture and long-term and not get stuck with a short-term "good enough" mindset was an easy trap to fall into. Would I be prepared to make radical decisions, seek out the best of the best, not settle for what I had, and make tough calls when needed? I wrestled intensely with the decision, as letting good people go felt cruel and unkind. When you are a small company that feels more like a family than a business, letting people go is exceptionally difficult. I cared deeply about each person on our team. Still, my business coach, whom I had recently started working with, reminded me, "Building great, big, impactful businesses is not about playing happy families. Instead, this process is akin to creating a winning professional sports team that can win championships and medals." This bit of advice helped clarify my thinking enormously. Could I build the best possible team by hiring top talent we didn't already have so we could become the fastest growing, market-leading, mission-driven, pioneering-glamping company the United States had seen? Would I have the confidence to bench some players and buy new players to bring in the talent we needed to go on the next leg of our journey? Could we significantly ramp up our pace of growth and professionalization of the business, moving from being a scrappy, chaotic, young company to becoming the organized, professional, strong brand I envisioned we could one day become? The short answer was yes! All this was possible, but it came with the price of making hard choices and saying some goodbyes.

For many women, one of the hardest parts of being the founder or CEO is making tough decisions around people, especially when people generally do a good job. When people are completely failing, it is a much easier decision, but when it's time to shift gears and make changes to build for the future, it is very hard. Yet, I have learned that when people can no longer do the job you need, it sends the wrong message to the rest of the team if we keep carrying a team member who is no longer optimal in their role. It is not kind to let people stay in a role where they can no longer succeed. We do people no service by carrying them when we should release them to go succeed somewhere else. Sometimes, therefore, kindness can look like letting people go.

I still feel sick to my stomach every time I need to have a hard conversation with someone, having made the tough call in my head to let them go. Those feelings never seem to go away, and, in some sense, I hope they never will. Feeling deeply uncomfortable about letting someone go reminds me that I am human and care about someone else's well-being, which means this is not a decision I have taken lightly or easily. If I've done my job well, however, no one should ever be surprised by this news as it will have been clear for some time if someone was no longer succeeding in their role. Communicating directly and openly not only sets your team members up for success, but also makes it easier when the time comes for you to say goodbye to those who are no longer the right fit.

No one will ever tell you they made a mistake letting someone go too quickly, but too many people will say they waited too long, or they didn't move fast enough when they knew things were awry. My motto is, "Hire slow and fire fast." I take my time in the hiring process to ensure I have the right fit, but I don't wait to act when I know someone needs to go. The challenge of leading teams requires me to put my big girl pants on and build the teams I need for each leg of my journey. When my business is hanging in the balance and the challenges I face seem insurmountable, I will only want a rock star team around me, a team who has not only bought into my vision, but is capable, committed, and able to scale every mountain with me.

The people you hire at the beginning of your journey may not necessarily be the people you will need later, and that's OK. It's normal. Some people can grow and develop at an exceptional rate and can be on the startup growth journey for a long time, taking different roles and responsibilities within the company and growing as the company grows. But it will likely be important to bring in new expertise to help you go on to the next leg of the journey, to help you tackle the next set of challenges you will inevitably encounter.

Team Building

Every new camp we ever opened always put our people under enormous strain, but camaraderie built in the literal trenches of overcoming difficult problems together cemented our people like glue. There was never a more compelling sense of actively building a team than when we were solving challenging problems together or fighting against tight deadlines. Seeing people rally around challenges and obstacles allowed our teams to flex their expertise and provided an opportunity for leaders to rise within our ranks.

When we opened our second camp in Montana in 2014, just outside Glacier National Park, local building authorities shut the camp down just days after we opened. We had been rallying to finish all the construction work for weeks, battling constant delays due to materials not arriving promptly and contractors walking off the job. Our team had been working night and day to erect all the tents, make everything functional as it should be, and get the last of the construction completed. We were immensely excited, as we were unveiling our newly designed tree house tent that would be unique to that camp. We thought sleeping among the treetops would be incredibly popular, so we had staked a lot of money on building that first unique tree house tent. However, within days of being open, an unexpected building inspector swung by the camp and declared that the tree house tent was not meeting the local building code and that all our other decked tents needed additional work to bring them up to code. Having already spent months battling with contractors, this was devastating news and not the ideal way to open our brand-new camp, as every day we were not open was costing us desperately needed revenue. Yet our on-the-ground team rallied together to fix every issue, pass every inspection, and get us back open again in record time. We might have gotten off to a false start, but overcoming those challenges cemented the team and enabled us to see the real leaders among them. Surprisingly, one of the housekeepers from that first season eventually became the camp's general manager as she demonstrated what an extraordinary leader she was, capable of solving problems, commanding her team's respect, and working together to overcome big challenges. Solving challenges together allowed leaders to rise and created a strong sense of team.

We need people around us who will rise to all the challenges we will face, and who will not only follow our leadership, but also take responsibility for solving the tough problems. We don't need to be everything to everyone, but we need to put together a team of people who will thrive together, especially under pressure.

Inspiring with Vision

Today, more than ever, hiring great people is exceptionally challenging. After the "great resignation" following the long years of the COVID-19 pandemic, employees are increasingly concerned about working for companies that have clear values, a strong sense of mission and purpose, and who recognize the importance of balance between home life and work life. This is where a startup can come into its own, because startups often can allow for a high degree of flexibility in exchange for passion, grit, and hard work. For a startup, it is vital to sell a vision of what the business will become and the excitement of making that vision happen, as well as communicating the company's purpose in the world. Therefore, founders need to be passionate people with a clear and compelling vision of what they want to achieve in the world. "You can be part of this crazy, amazing dream of building something extraordinary that's not been done before! Come and be part of where we're going!" The people who joined us in our early days bought into a dream, feeling they could contribute to a bigger purpose, connecting with something deserving of their energy and effort. Startups rarely have much to offer in the way of salary or benefits, so being able to inspire people with something they can be passionate about and contribute toward is essential. Don't underestimate what people will be prepared to sacrifice or give up in exchange for purpose, passion, and vision; don't underestimate the strong desire to see great leadership. In 2022, a survey revealed that 82 percent of people would consider quitting a job because of a bad manager or leader.[1] Our responsibility to lead well, therefore, has never been more critical.

Great leadership means being out in front of your people, determining where you are going, providing a clear vision, and communicating with your team what it will take. As our team increases in size, it can become increasingly difficult to maintain the same level of interactions with our teammates and harder to ensure everyone has all the information they need. How do we enable everyone to stay on the same page as our company grows? When you and a handful of people gathered around your kitchen table, it's easy to share your vision and divvy up responsibilities. But as my team expanded and I was no longer directly managing everyone, town halls became an exceptionally useful way of sharing and imparting strategy and vision. Usually held once a month, a town hall is a gathering (online or in person) for all employees, regardless of their role, to get together and hear what is going on in the business, to be inspired again by the company's mission and vision, and to create space for employees to ask questions, seek clarification, and bring critique when needed. I found these gatherings to be the perfect moment to recognize our employees of the month and reward employees who reflected our company values and were going above and beyond. It was also a great forum to credit specific people or teams needing recognition. Those gatherings were always a moment for us to step out of our day-to-day responsibilities, step back and see the bigger picture, see what was happening across departments, and understand how we were progressing toward hitting our goals. It was always good to be reminded of our bigger vision, why we were working so hard, and what we contributed to building. Casting that vision and reminding people of it at least monthly was a critical aspect of leading the team and building a strong sense of unity. Those gatherings were also usually my favorite time of the month. They were the times I felt most connected to our team and the most open and honest about everything happening. I've cried in distress in town halls. I've inspired, rallied, answered criticism, and handled backlash. I've calmed troubled waters and gained insight I wouldn't have had otherwise. I always stood as a peer but rose as a leader amongst our people. Gathering our people together that way was always a privilege and honor.

Showcasing Your Team

Investors expect to see founders surrounding themselves with talented people who are capable problem solvers, bought into the vision, and capable of going on the journey ahead. This page in the pitch deck outlines the key people in the business—those key team members going on this big journey with you to make great things happen. We don't need to highlight all our team members on this page, but our key leaders and strategic advisory support should be showcased. We want to show that our business is more than just me spinning plates and that we've invested in people to help make things happen. No business on a path to becoming big can be a one-person show. By focusing solely on our combined contributions and skills, we can avoid reinforcing the perception that we are a small business destined to stay small. Building a winning team that can execute ambitious goals, tackle significant challenges, and drive growth is crucial. The possibilities of what we can achieve are greatly influenced by the people around the table and what we can accomplish together.

When investors look at your team, they are thinking about execution risk. Do you have the right people on the bus to execute your vision? Is this a winning, well-rounded team capable of pulling off something extraordinary? Are there any people gaps? Who will they need to hire to help solve some of the big challenges ahead? Thinking about what key hires you will make with investment capital coming into the business will also help alleviate investor concerns. Demonstrating who you need next and who is essential for your next growth season is critical in demonstrating you understand where your company is today and that you can lead the team to execute your vision, taking the business to the next level.

In addition to the internal team, this page can showcase any mentors or advisors working with you. If anyone in your corner has been there, done it before, and is guiding, directing, and helping you, you can also mention them. The presence of advisors can create additional confidence and indicates you are willing to learn, take advice, and get support from people who may be more experienced than you.

Surrounding yourself with outstanding people is what this page in the pitch deck is all about. Thinking about showcasing your team on the page should make us think about the kind of team we are building. One of the biggest shifts women must make to transition from building a small business to building a big business comes from the necessity of building a strategic team of talented, outstanding people. To do that, we must throw off our scarcity of mentalities that say there isn't enough time or money to do so. When we think there isn't enough of something, we trap ourselves. We get stuck thinking we need to perform all the roles in our business and we don't hire the necessary expertise to enable the business to grow beyond ourselves. That mindset keeps us playing a small game and carrying the world on our shoulders. We cannot build big businesses by ourselves. It is simply not possible. We must stop thinking it all depends on us and start acting like it depends on the people we hire to sit at our table.

Investors are looking at the founder and whether they are successfully building the team needed to scale the business. Without a talented team, your business will only become as big as you can manage, which will invariably mean it will stay small. We can't afford not to hire great people; we don't have time to waste doing everything ourselves. So don't hold back; make smart investments in people and empower your team to build what you can imagine.

Painting a picture of what is yet to come and taking our team on a journey to realize that vision is a crucial underlying factor in building a high-performing team and scaling a business. We must lead our people with a clear vision to make the impossible possible. Are you building the team you need today for the company you can imagine tomorrow?

Questions for Reflection

- What's holding you back from building your team? Are you suffering from a scarcity mentality? Are you thinking too small, placing too much emphasis on yourself to solve all your challenges, and filling too many roles?
- Who is the next most critical hire in your business? What value do you expect them to bring to the table?
- What is your definition of a rock star for your team?
- Have you defined and communicated what success looks like for each role in your company? Have you got reasonable expectations?
- Is your team clear on what goals you are trying to achieve and what initiatives you are embracing to try and achieve those goals?
- How good are you at holding people accountable?
- What is your biggest takeaway as you reflect on the status of your current team? In what ways do you need to act?

Slide Nine of the Pitch Deck: Team

Showcase the key people in your team. Include a headshot of each person, their title in your company, and any relevant, pertinent experience or background to quickly indicate who everyone is. If investors can quickly gain insight into the background or experience of your team, they can get clarity regarding the caliber and quality of the team. Advisors and mentors can also be showcased in the same way, but ideally, do not have more than two to three advisors on the page. This page should predominantly showcase the outstanding, talented team you have assembled.

9

Asking for Funding and Getting It

Ask not what your country can do for you— ask what you can do for your country.

—John F. Kennedy

After nearly a year of pitching investors and having countless conversations that led nowhere, I was introduced to a venture capital firm that loved the travel space and what we were building. They invited me to pitch them in person and to meet their whole team. I was incredibly nervous, but better prepared this time than I had been previously. I knew my financial performance metrics and was well-versed in investor speak by now. I knew the questions they would ask me, and I was ready. I was ready to give the pitch of my life and win them over.

The meeting was a big success, and not long after that meeting, they made us an offer, giving us a term sheet outlining all the terms and conditions for that offer. I was elated and relieved that finally, after months and months of pitching, my efforts were paying off. I thought I had done it and secured the future of my business with the promise of a seven-million-dollar capital injection into our fledgling company. The company desperately needed money to keep growing and building financial stability in order to move away from the financial knife edge we had been living on for the last seven years. However, the term sheet was complex and read like gobbledygook. It contained legal terminology I did not understand, and I have a law degree! We hired corporate lawyers to explain the terms and help us negotiate. I was again out of my depth and nervous.

The term sheet for seven million dollars was more money than I had originally asked for when I made my pitch. The investors thought I would need more money than my request, which was correct, so it was generous in its amount. But despite this generosity, the terms required us to drastically reduce our ownership stake in the company, giving up a large amount of the company to the investors in exchange for their investment. In addition, an enormous amount of power would be in their hands, leaving us with little control of our company. They were planning to come in and take a minority share of the business, meaning they would own less than 50 percent of the company, but were also asking for their shares to have preference over ours. This means their shares would, in effect, be returned to them at three times their original value before we received anything. The terms felt predatory and less than ideal. We tried to negotiate with them for better terms for weeks, as the last thing I wanted to do was let this deal go. It had taken so long to reach this point that the thought of turning the offer down seemed absurd. We were also running out of time as our cash was disappearing by the day, making us desperately close to running completely out of money. Given our precarious position, it was so tempting to just take the deal. It was a terrifying moment. I could see the payroll looming and had no idea how I would pay all our expenses that month, even though I had a seven-million-dollar offer on the table.

However, I could not escape the feeling that I was not only underselling my business but also selling my soul if I did this deal. These investors had valued my company at a much lower valuation than I knew other companies like mine were being valued. I felt that my male counterparts were getting a better deal. I had a business that was generating significant revenue and was profitable, yet my offer was low.

At the same time as all this was happening, I was opening a new camp. We had signed a contract to purchase a piece of land that would be the home of our next camp, but on closing day, our seller disappeared. Despite being under contract to sell to us, he got cold feet and wanted to back out. I had a sinking feeling in the pit of my belly. It was another thing I had to talk to our potential investors about. I immediately called them and said, "This has happened; I am sorting it out; I have lawyers, I think we have a good contract, and I think we can force him to close, but it is a bit messy. It is not great. But I will sort it out. I will deal with it."

The investor who offered me the seven million term sheet replied, "Well, that's very bad for you. That's very, very bad for you. If you don't sort that out, that will look very bad and be on you. You will have many consequences if you don't work that out."

His aggressive, bully-like response was the final straw, giving me the impetus to pull the plug on the deal. I called the investor back the next day, thanked him for his time, and shared that we wouldn't be moving forward with the deal. He replied, "If you don't do this deal, no one will give you any money, and I'll ensure it. I will blackball you in the venture capitalist (VC) world, and you will never raise money from anyone." The intimidation was intense, but I realized that I didn't need that kind of person on my board, and if I wasn't certain about turning this deal down before, I was now.

I wanted investors who had my back, who would support me when hard things happened, and who would encourage, offer advice, and champion me through stressful times. I didn't need someone who would bully me, threaten me, and cause me more stress than I was already experiencing. I longed for him to ask me, "How can I help? What do you need?" I realized this investor was not that person and that he was not the person with whom I wanted to partner. I already wanted to divorce him, and we weren't married yet. I knew I had to decline the offer.

I cried and shared the news with our staff at our monthly town hall meeting. I didn't just cry; I stood before everyone and sobbed. I couldn't keep in the overwhelming emotions and the distress I felt, having reached this point yet unable to get the deal over the line. It was so disappointing, and everyone felt it. But this moment galvanized our company values. For the first time, I had complete clarity regarding our company values. I knew I couldn't let anyone on board who didn't share those values and was not interested in standing alongside us shoulder to shoulder in the business. Just like hiring employees for great "culture fit," I knew I needed investors who were also a great fit and who were prepared to not over-inflate their importance and value and devalue my team and me. I realized I didn't need to give in to intimidation or compromise my values or sense of worth by listening to someone who was potentially incredibly powerful, but who was not valuing me or seeing my worth. It's so common that we want other people to validate us and indicate our worth, but it is up to each one of us not to be dependent on other people's opinions of us or actions toward us to dictate that worth. We must find our sense of worth deep inside and believe in ourselves. We must value ourselves and what we bring to the table. We must set the agenda for putting a dollar figure on our heads. For sure we, of course, must listen to what the market will bear, but we don't need to let anyone belittle us, speak down to us, or treat us poorly. We need a keen sense of self. Otherwise, the world will walk all over us.

That moment bolstered my sense of self and gave me increasing courage to stand up for myself as my entire team rallied around to support me, picking me up from that moment of crisis and giving me the determination to find another way forward.

After we turned down this predatory offer, our company was back at the drawing board, but I had not given up. I knew there had to be a way through this unending fundraising nightmare. There had to be people out there who aligned with our values. That's when I realized I had only encountered one female investor during that entire year while meeting investors. Right then, I decided that if I ever managed to sell my company, I would start investing in female entrepreneurs. I would become the investor I had been looking for. That was fine, but I still needed to find someone to open the door for me and write a check to help me grow my business so I had a chance to build a valuable company that could be sold.

This was the moment when I realized there was a second pathway that could help me connect to capital. The first path required me to get warm introductions to investors from people I knew or had met to get directly in front of venture capitalists. This phenomenon fundamentally discriminates, relying on founders being well-networked and connected with the right people. For women and people of color, these social networks simply do not exist, perpetuating the 'white boys club' in the venture funding space, making it much harder for women and people of color to get funded. However, an alternative pathway to getting in front of investors became apparent. For a fee, brokers and investment bankers can help make those all-important introductions on behalf of founders, helping them leapfrog across the social network divide.

Introductions

Even though I knew that in almost all other industries brokers exist to help connect us to the resources we need, this option did not seem obvious to me. Brokers help us find the right insurance products, mortgages, and credit cards; why not fund a business? Finding the right funding proved a full-time job—could a broker or an investment banker help me cut through the mud I was stuck in and connect me to the right financial resources?

I received an unexpected email a few weeks after I had turned the VC term sheet down saying, "I think we can help you raise capital." At this point, I was tired and ready to try anything. I replied to the email, and within a week, the broker had flown up to meet me and discuss who and what kind of funding might be the right fit for us. I had no idea such a service existed, but it was one of the best resources I have ever used. The broker was able to take a holistic look at our business and what was performing well and what we were trying to achieve long-term to ensure that he found the right fit for us—the right type of capital, and the right amount. I discovered that an equity investment or an exchange of capital for shares in the business was not the only way investors were willing to invest in businesses. We discovered that a combination deal that included some equity and debt was the right formula for our business, given that we had good cash flow and could service some debt. This was ideal for us as it meant we did not have to give away a huge percentage of our company and give up a large degree of control. We ended up giving up a much smaller piece of equity in our company and taking on a larger amount of debt into the business, consolidating all our existing bank and credit card debt into one new, larger debt facility with a new lender. No more credit card juggling for me! Even though using a broker cost us a success fee (typically 1.5 percent of the capital raise), it was well spent to help us get the right capital into our business.

Within months, we received a term sheet for thirty million dollars instead of the seven million dollars we had been offered originally, and we only had to give away a fraction of the company. We found partners who, to this day, have been supportive, helpful, and generous with their time and advice. They were an all-male team investing in our family-owned business but they were the kind of investors you want to call in a pinch. Investors I still consider friends and who I know care about me and my family as much as they do about making money. They were a great fit.

Types of Funding

Understanding that there wasn't just one type of funding was critical in getting the right capital from the right people into our company. Understanding all of the funding options and mastering the meaning of complicated investment terms increased my ability to negotiate and do a good deal for me and the investor. Win-win scenarios make everyone happy. Understanding what a bad deal looked like helped me realize that just because someone offers you money doesn't mean you have to take it. There isn't just one type of investor or type of money; there's a smorgasbord, and it's important to get the right fit for you.

Let's explore together some of the most widely used investment terms and types of capital available to rapidly scaling businesses.

Equity Deals

An equity deal is the typical type of funding a venture capitalist would utilize to invest in a company. An amount of capital is invested in exchange for company shares after determining its current value. This concept is simple in principle, but some nuances are worth understanding.

Preference Shares

There can be several distinct types of shares that shareholders can have. Founders usually have common stock—a normal type of stock. In contrast, venture capitalists often desire preferred stock or shares, meaning their shares are preferred over any common stock. When an investor has preference stock, they may or may not receive an interest payment paid on their money annually and they will receive certain preferred rights over common shareholders. Unlike common shares, preference shares have certain preferential treatment regarding dividend payments and other rights. Preference shares can often have a 2× or 3× liquidation preference compared with common shares. In simple terms, that means that upon a liquidation event, or the sale of the company, the preferred shareholders would get their money back two or three times before common shareholders receive anything. This is a way for investors to insulate themselves against negative events and to guarantee their return. Do you remember how I said earlier that early-stage VC funds are looking for a 10× return on their money? Ensuring they have preference shares is a way to minimize their risk and increase their likelihood of a return, particularly in a downside scenario. The downside of an investor having preference shares is that if they have significant preference shares, they could make a lot more money than you on a potential exit, or their preference share could diminish your return. Let's examine this example to help unpack this further.

If an investor invests $5 million into start-up A for a 20 percent equity stake with a 1× preference and that start-up was sold for $10 million, the investor would make a $5 million return, and the remaining shareholders would make

$5 million. The investor would effectively get 50 percent of the value because of their preference. If that start-up sells for $25 million, that investor would still make $5 million, and the remaining shareholders would make $20 million. Only when a company hits a certain valuation does that preference have no diminishing effect on the remaining shareholders. Let's examine what happens, however, if an investor invests with a 3x preference.

An investor invests $5 million into start-up B for a 20 percent equity stake with a 3x preference. If the start-up is sold for $10 million, the investor would receive all of the proceeds, as their preference threshold would not have been hit. The remaining shareholders would receive nothing because the company valuation would not be high enough to meet the investors' contracted return threshold. When the business was sold, they would receive all the proceeds, as their shares would take preference. If the company is sold for $25 million, the investor would make $15 million, and $10 million would go to the remaining shareholders. The investor would receive almost two-thirds of the proceeds despite only owning 20 percent of the shares.

In comparison, if all shareholders have common stock, and an investor invests $5 million dollars into start-up C for a 20 percent equity stake, and the company sells for $10 million, the investor would receive $2 million (less than the $5 million they invested) and the remaining shareholders would receive $8 million.

This balancing act of protecting capital entering a business is why preference shares exist. The mechanism is designed to protect investors from low-valuation exit outcomes, ensuring they can protect their capital and make a return in such a scenario. However, the higher the preference, the more likely they become overly punitive and unfair toward the founders and other common shareholders. Therefore, it is a good idea to run some hypothetical exit outcomes for your business and consider what valuation you think might be possible so you can understand at what point preference shares would become non-impactful and where they would be punitive.

It is acceptable for investors to have 1x or 1.5x preference shares, and we commonly see 2x preferences in the market too. However, 3x or more preferences should be considered unreasonable unless you are confident that you are on a trajectory that will make the preference not an issue. I recently saw a term sheet for one of the companies I'm invested in with a 5x preference, so investors are making big asks. But we shouldn't be afraid to hold our ground and turn down deals that aren't in our best interest. In some cases, preference shares may also include voting rights separate from common shareholders, giving them specific powers to control the company in certain ways, even if they have a minority shareholding position. For example, preference shareholders may have the right to veto certain matters, such as changes to the company's charter or the issuance of additional shares.

SAFE Notes

Simple agreement for future equity (SAFE) notes are a way for your investors to receive a specific number of shares at an agreed-upon price in the future, usually when your start-up raises another round of funding. SAFE notes are common for early-stage individual investors investing five hundred thousand dollars or less. Instead of having to determine the current value of the company and take a percentage of the company as shares as described above, a SAFE note will guarantee them a certain number of shares later when the company raises a larger amount of money (known as a round) when another investor sets the valuation price. Typically, SAFE note investors get a discount on the company's future valuation, effectively rewarding them for investing earlier than a priced round. A valuation cap, or ceiling price, of the company may also be provided in the SAFE note. This allows the investor to invest at a lower valuation than the next round of funding ascribes.

For example, if when future capital is raised and the company is valued at ten million dollars, the SAFE note holder would be able to invest at the pre-determined valuation cap amount or an agreed discounted amount (e.g., $4 million) instead of the new valuation amount (e.g., $10 million). The number of shares the SAFE noteholder would get would be equivalent to the lower valuation. They would be rewarded with more shares at a lower valuation because they invested early and didn't record their shares immediately.

The benefits of this type of mechanism for both founders and investors are that they are typically quick to negotiate and execute, which reduces the time and cost of getting a deal done. A lot of time does not need to be spent determining the company's value, and a simple one- or two-page agreement can be drawn up and signed quickly. Many standard templates for SAFE notes can be used for this purpose. Investors benefit from a lower valuation rate when future money is brought into the company, giving them more shares than they would have potentially had if investing in that round, and founders can access capital more quickly and easily. When the time comes to raise more money, early-stage investors will benefit from the heavy lifting done by other investors who will set the company's valuation.

Understanding the Small Print

Equity deals often come with what most of us would call "small print." Understanding how something works and what's considered standard and not standard gives you the power to make informed choices. Doing the math on any deal presented to you is important in conjunction with having an experienced lawyer explain the complex terms and conditions presented to you. A lawyer who has negotiated other term sheets for other founders and can reflect to you what is current and normal at that time will be hugely helpful. However, never ignore your intuition. If your lawyer tells you (as mine did) that the terms presented are normal and reasonable in the market, but you still don't feel good about them, don't take them. Only you can determine what feels reasonable and like a good deal. Just because someone offers you money doesn't mean you must take it. You need to figure out how to get the money markets to work for you on terms that make sense.

After meeting our broker, I realized I could do a different deal. It made much more sense when the broker told me I could put a large amount of debt into my business instead of doing an all-equity deal (cash into the business in exchange for shares). Rather than giving away large amounts of the company at a low valuation, we could afford to take on some non-dilutive debt because we had a cash-flowing business and could make interest payments. We decided to do a debt and equity deal where we gave away a small number of shares in the business in exchange for cash into the business, and in addition, we took on a large amount of debt that would need to be repaid.

Debt Deals

Over the last few years, while working with female founders, I've noticed that women, in general, tend to be much more averse to the risk of debt than the idea of taking an equity injection. Even though, logically, the cost of debt can potentially be infinitely lower than giving away huge chunks of your company in an equity deal, women still fear the risk of debt. The responsibility of knowing that you must pay back the capital in a particular time frame and make regular interest payments seems to make women nervous even though we have been taking loans to buy homes and cars for a long time. The risk of debt associated with the possibility of being unable to make payments and, therefore, going bankrupt seems to make women afraid and more hesitant to embrace these risks. However, that fear is often just one way we sell ourselves short; we reduce our potential upside later when we take less risk up front and limit the growth and wealth we could have achieved. We see this even in small businesses when women consistently use less debt than men to grow their businesses. Women typically have greater unmet credit needs than men, with women less likely to apply for loans when needed and more likely to put off decisions to promote their growth.[1] The historical lack of access to capital has undoubtedly contributed to the conditioning of female thinking around debt and the associated risks. Women have forgotten to think about the opportunity cost of not doing something and over-valued the risk of doing something. It is time to start rebalancing that thinking and understand what options are open to us. I was able to make that leap in my head when I realized just how predatory venture investors can be. Taking on more debt suddenly seemed much less risky than having an aggressive, unhelpful investor at the table. Taking on debt was also much less risky than having no cash injection into our business.

If your business produces cash flow, you should consider debt as an option to help you grow your business. If you do not have any free cash flow just yet, then the debt will not be an option until you do since you will need cash in the business to make monthly interest payments to service the debt. Occasionally, debt providers will allow you to use the borrowed money to service the interest due, but only in the short term and in certain circumstances. For our purposes, therefore, our starting point is this: Do you have cash flow? If yes, let's consider the types of debt available.

Traditional Bank Debt

The first type of debt is traditional bank debt, which requires collateral in your business to secure a loan. That could be an asset in the business or a large order from a buyer that the bank may provide invoice financing for. The thing to remember is banks like security and will be looking for a way to secure the loan they want to give you against an asset of some kind. That asset might even be your future revenue, like the scenario of financing a large order you've received. You may need cash to manufacture or service that order; a bank loan could meet that need.

Mezzanine Debt

When you don't have any collateral, the bank can't use it to secure the debt; an unsecured form called mezzanine debt might be possible. Lacking traditional collateral to secure the loan means the debt provider will instead typically take a pledge of your shares in the company to secure their debt. Your shares in the company will be pledged to the debt provider until the debt is repaid, and in the event you can't repay the debt, the provider can take possession of your shares in the company to facilitate paying themselves back. Given that this is riskier for the debt provider, this kind of debt is more expensive, typically costing anywhere from 11 to 18 percent per year, depending on the underlying base interest rate. While this sounds expensive, it might not be as expensive as giving away 20 to 30 percent of your company or your VC investor having 3× preference shares.

Once you decide on the ideal type of capital for your business, communicate it to investors. Decide whether you want a debt, an equity deal, or a combination of the two.

Valuations

The financial markets will always tell you what the going rate for something is, your start-up included, because investors will tell you what they are willing to pay. The price of anything is always determined by what the market is willing to pay. Unfortunately, I frequently see founders making the mistake of trying to set the valuation of their company themselves by pitching investors, as we see on hit TV shows like *Shark Tank* or *Dragon's Den*. Things like, "I'm asking for an investment of $100,000 for 10 percent of my company." Let's be clear: while that makes great TV, I don't believe it's a great real-world tactic, largely because the deals we see getting done on TV never actually get done quite that simply or cleanly. Knowing how much of your company you are willing to give away in exchange for investment is helpful. Still, founders will often make the mistake of inappropriately pricing their start-up, overinflating the value in the early days and undervaluing the company in later years. I think it's smarter to let the financial markets determine what the market is willing to pay so you don't shoot yourself in the foot by either over or under-valuing yourself. The demand for something will drive up the price and vice versa. Because investors are always looking at many deals, comparing like businesses, and seeing what other investors are doing, they have a great sense of how things are priced. General financial market conditions also greatly impact how companies are valued and what valuations investors can offer. When capital flows freely in the market, valuations tend to be higher. When there is more hesitancy and nervousness in the financial markets, such as in times of recession, pandemics, or high inflation, valuations tend to be lower. It's impossible for a founder to understand all these nuances and to value themselves appropriately. Therefore, it is smarter not to even try and instead allow the markets to tell you what they are willing to pay. Once you know the market's valuation, you can negotiate accordingly.

Entrepreneurs often ask me things like, "What formula is used to calculate a valuation?" The reality is that there are a myriad of ways to think about valuation: applying a multiple to your earnings, before interest, taxes, depreciation, and amortization (EBITDA) number or discounting your cashflow and working backward from where we believe your company will be in five to seven years to determine what price can be paid today are just two of the most common methods. However, even in applying basic formulaic principles, the markets, and specifically how confident the financial markets are and how much capital is flowing in those markets, will influence valuation. Suppose your business is in an emerging market, for example, on the African continent. In that case, it is likely to be valued differently than a business at the same stage in the United States. Market volatility, currency devaluation, country risk, and ease of doing business will all influence valuation. For these reasons and more, appropriately valuing companies can be challenging. Founders should focus on getting their ask right instead of worrying about valuation.

Defining Your Ask

Your entire pitch deck has led to this moment. The unqualified purpose of your pitch deck's preceding pages is to successfully position your ask to investors on this final page. There are three critical elements for every ask:

1. X is the amount of money that I need
2. Y is how I plan to spend it
3. Z is how it will enable us to grow.

Founders often make an ask, but they forget to communicate what they plan to do with the investment or how much growth the investment will help achieve.

It's easy to say, "I need one million dollars," or to simply pluck a number out of thin air. It's much harder to say, "I need one million dollars, and with it, I will do A, B, and C and subsequently turn the investment into D."

On this page, you need to demonstrate that you understand the drivers of putting capital to work effectively and strategically and that you are clear about what you need and why you need it. Asking for the right amount of capital is your starting point. Understanding what stage your business is at is the key to this. Have you raised capital before? How much revenue are you doing? If you are at the idea stage, haven't generated any revenue, and you ask for five million dollars, you are unlikely to be successful. Pre-revenue companies or companies at the ideation stage are what we call pre-seed companies, who, at most, can raise twenty-five thousand dollars to five hundred thousand dollars from angels, accelerator programs, or early-stage investors. Only when you have some traction, a product showing some product-market fit, and you have moved beyond just being an idea can you consider raising a seed round.

In a seed round, founders can raise between $200,000 and $2 million, depending on traction to date and trajectory. Those funds do not necessarily need to be raised all in one go. We often see founders raising a seed cash injection and then another and maybe another to help bridge them through to raising their next priced round of funding. SAFE notes would likely allow investors to put subsequent seed checks into the business. Through my fund, I invest in founders at this seed stage, writing checks between $200,000 and $1 million to female founders who are doing at least $50,000 in revenue already and are on a trajectory to do $1 million in revenue in the next year to eighteen months. That million-dollar trajectory is critical because that's the floor for raising a Series A, the next round of funding after your seed round. If you are doing $1 million in revenue, you are eligible to raise a Series A round, where you could raise anywhere from $2 million to $10 million. After that round, the series continues: B, C, and D, and as the milestones get larger, so do the check sizes.

In summary, the stages of a business's life cycle correlating to funding cycles are as follows:

- Pre-seed: often pre-revenue or doing under $50,000 in revenue. Able to raise $10,000 to $500,000 in capital
- Seed stage: often doing between $50,000 and $1 million in revenue. Able to raise $200,000 to $2 million in capital

- Series A: typically doing more than $1 million in revenue. Able to raise $2 million to $10 million.
- Series B and beyond: typically have raised previous capital and are generating more revenue than the Series A requirement

If you can identify your stage, you can position your ask correctly to the right kind of investors who invest at your stage, and you can ask for an appropriate amount. Investors typically invest in specific stages of a business's life cycle because they believe they can add the most value at that stage or are comfortable with the risk and return profile of companies. Knowing your stage helps you ask for the right amount from the right people. Even if you know you will need more money soon, investors will struggle to reconcile writing larger checks when you've not shown you've met the criteria for being a later-stage business. Recognize your stage and do the work to understand what it will take to level up your business to the next stage. Your next challenge is demonstrating to investors how you will use their capital to drive your growth.

Capital Should Drive Growth

I love seeing founders break down their capital and ask how they will use those funds, but even more critically, investors want to know what founders are hoping to achieve by receiving investment. Investors want to see how you think investing capital in specific ways will move the needle and propel your business forward. Of course, you don't have to be completely accurate with your predictions; no one is going to hold your feet to the fire if you spend one-hundred-thousand dollars on marketing instead of the fifty-thousand dollars you thought you would, but investors want to see that you've thought about generating return on investment (ROI). We all know the financial needs of our businesses can be all-consuming, never-ending sinkholes for cash, but that's where we must get smarter, because capital is currently not easy to come by for female founders. How can we, therefore, make a little capital go a long way? How can we use capital to get us as far as we can? How can we leverage debt to make our cash in the business go further? It's not enough to simply say, for example, we will spend one-hundred-thousand dollars on better manufacturing equipment. We've got to say we need new manufacturing equipment to help us increase production and lower our cost of production, increasing our margins. You need to spend capital on initiatives that will improve your business, move you forward, and, most critically, help you reach the next milestones to either help you raise more capital or enable you to become profitable. If we don't do those things, we risk getting stuck, being unable to raise more capital, and unable to get to profitability—we want to avoid getting stuck at all costs.

Capital is Fuel

It's important to remember that all money is expensive in one way or another. Still, costly capital is much better than having no money and no opportunities to drive growth and create wealth. Putting money into your business is necessary if you want to fuel growth unless you already have a wildly profitable, cash-producing business. The questions you need to ask yourself are what type of capital (debt, equity, or a hybrid) and how much capital you need. Understanding the options available to you and the kind of capital that is right for your growth strategy is fundamental to achieving the growth you want for your business. Be clear on what you are asking for and why, and how that amount of capital will help propel your business to grow exponentially.

Questions for Reflection

- What fears do you have about bringing capital into your business? Do those fears hold you back from making an ask? What do you need to do to circumvent those fears?
- What stage of life is your business at? Pre-seed, seed, series A, B, or beyond?
- How much capital do you believe is the right amount to ask for? Does this amount correlate with the stage that you are at?
- Are you clear on how you are going to use the funds to fuel your growth? What impact do you think this capital will have on your business? What ROI do you think it will create?
- Can you connect the dots between the amount you are asking for and what you hope to achieve because of this capital injection?
- When thinking about your ask, what makes you feel intimidated or uncertain?

- On a scale of one to ten, how confident are you feeling about making your ask? What could you do to improve your confidence if you didn't score yourself a ten?

Slide Ten of the Pitch Deck: Ask

On this final page of your pitch deck, include the following:

- How much you are asking for, and whether you are asking for equity, debt, or both.
- What you will spend that money on—a pie chart is a nice way to break the funding into different spending buckets.
- Tell us, in one or two lines, your expectations around how you expect the capital to propel you forward or help you hit specific milestones.

10

The World Is Waiting for You

No one can stop us. We will speak for our rights and we will bring change through our voice. We must believe in the power and the strength of our words. Our words can change the world.

—Malala Yousafzai

As a child, I was brought up on a diet of fairy tales where the eponymous princess waited for the sword-wielding, charismatic Prince Charming to rescue her. The fairy tales were instrumental in conveying the overarching message of patriarchy: women were meant to be beautiful, coy, patient, and rescued. When I watched *Star Wars* for the first time, Princess Leia stood as a jarring contrast to that message. She immediately became my hero, with her iconic braided hair and all. Her character refused to conform to the role of playing the damsel in distress, instead portraying a very different kind of princess. In the scene where Han Solo and Luke Skywalker sneak into the Death Star to "rescue" Princess Leia, she refuses to sit back demurely, waiting for the men to finish off the enemy. Had she relied on them for protection, they would have perished. Leia quickly picks up the gun and fires while mocking Han when he accidentally blocks their only escape route: "This is some rescue!" Leia tells him before shooting open an escape passage. "Somebody has to save our skin," she continues, implying that she was the one who finally would.

Leia's character introduced a paradigm shift that challenged what all girls were conditioned to believe. Instead of waiting for someone else to solve the problems of our day or make important things happen, we can take on tough challenges. We can be women wielding our metaphorical lightsabers, tackling systemic issues, taking down empires, and making big things happen. We can build incredible businesses that transform our communities, cities, nations, and world. We simply must trade in our outdated ways of looking at the world, dismantle the mindsets that hold us back and keep us living small lives, and embrace new self-perceptions and ways of thinking.

As I've worked alongside other female founders during the last five years, the most notable challenges that women face are not actually how hard it is to raise capital or how hard it is to scale and grow a multi-million-dollar business, even though those things are hard. The biggest challenges lie within our hearts and minds, where our limited expectations and pre-conditioned mindsets reside. These conditioned ideas are the stumbling blocks holding women back, causing us to live smaller lives than the world needs us to live. As Brené Brown would advocate, it's time we start "rumbling the stories in our own heads."[1] We need to recognize the mindsets that hold us back. Just as the early suffragettes reframed the position of women in society, arguing for equal voting rights, and the feminist movement of the 1960s created monumental shifts for women, sparking demands for equal opportunities, equal responsibilities, and equal pay, it is time we throw off the old ways of living and thinking that have kept us trapped against the glass ceilings that collectively confine and hold women back. We've explored numerous mindsets throughout this book that we've connected to the challenges of building a big business. To conclude, let's revisit and explore some of the most crippling thinking holding women back today.

Women and Wealth

Let's say it straight. There's still a pervasive mindset in our world today that says, "Women shouldn't be big wealth creators. Women shouldn't aim to be wealthy. Women are not worthy of wealth." There is still a huge stigma around the idea of women making a lot of money, that somehow it's inappropriate for women to be wealthy, that they do not deserve to be rewarded highly for their efforts, and that they are not worthy of wealth. This implies that women shouldn't be too ambitious, shouldn't dream big, and certainly shouldn't be making millions of dollars or building billion-dollar companies. For generations, it's been acceptable for women to build charitable organizations—the only thing women were permitted to do at one point. Women founding and building Fortune 500 companies from their inception is a less-imagined reality. But why shouldn't we be the main contributors to the world's wealth? Why shouldn't we not only imagine it but also do it? Not only is it just as appropriate for women to build valuable enterprises, but it's also critical that we do. Capital will only be managed more equally when women are also the ones creating and making significant wealth. Only when both men and women are equally financially powerful, when both sexes have equal access to wealth and equal power to leverage that wealth, will we start to see many more of the ills in our world disappear. Like Princess Leia, we must recognize that we are not damsels in distress waiting for someone else to rescue us and that we are the answer to many of the world's problems; it is our time to rebuild our world one business at a time. We don't need to temper our ambitions or scale back our ideas to make them more acceptable and normal.

The world needs radical women who are not afraid to lead, not afraid to think big, not afraid to smash ceilings, and normalize building world-class, incredibly valuable businesses. Let's stop imagining that we are not worthy or don't deserve it. Let's stop feeling embarrassed for thinking big. Let's normalize hearing women say, "I'm building a billion-dollar company." Let's expect stories proclaiming a female victory instead of being surprised. May those stories become so numerous that they are no longer noteworthy stories. Let's stop playing small games and start thinking about how we can and should build wealth. Let's stand on the shoulders of the women who have gone before us and reach for the stars they made possible for us to reach.

While we all know there is a long way to go in the fight for gender equality, today, we can vote in an election, we can own our bank accounts, we can have our credit cards, and we can pursue any profession we wish, all thanks to the struggles of women who went before us. Let's not squander those hard-won rights by playing small. Let's not be embarrassed to dream big and be ambitious, and let's realize that there is room at the table for all of us, even if we do have to build our own tables.

Women and Scarcity

The fear many women feel when another woman succeeds demonstrates that many of us operate with a scarcity mentality. Fearing the lack of seats at the table often manifests itself in a mindset that fears other women have taken our seats at the table. However, the fact that someone else has achieved something extraordinary doesn't mean there is no room for me. She hasn't taken my seat; her success doesn't diminish the possibility of my success. We don't need to think that there's only one female seat at the table or that only one woman can build a multi-million-dollar business. Instead, we must consider filling big tables and building new ones. When asked, "When will there be enough women on the Supreme Court?" Ruth Bader Ginsberg famously replied, "When there are nine! There's been nine men, and nobody's ever raised a question about that!"[2]

There isn't only one seat available; women are not competing for a limited number of seats. We don't need to be jealous of or diminished by other women's achievements. Instead, we must celebrate each victory as our own and keep holding our hands out to pull each other up. I frequently joke with my fellow investor and soon-to-be doctorate holder, Lelemba Phiri, who helped me pioneer Enygma Ventures in Africa, that she is currently getting a PhD for both of us. In turn, she likes to say that she has also built a 100-million-dollar company because I built one. Her success is my success; my success is also hers. Despite what the world would have us believe, there is plenty of room for all of us to succeed. There is plenty of opportunity to build upon each other's achievements and go further because a woman is already sitting at that table.

We don't need to shrink back. Instead, we need to pull up other chairs or go build more tables for us all to sit at. Having one woman already at the table doesn't mean there isn't room for you as well. Let's not let scarcity scare us into thinking we compete with other women. That mindset also keeps us stuck thinking small and pitted against each other instead of helping each other rise and leveraging each other as fuel. We must support and champion other fierce women, and we must surround ourselves with women who will do the same and have our backs.

Women Who Don't Play It Safe

Women have been conditioned to not only play it small but also play it safe. It's infinitely more comfortable staying in our comfort zones, where we feel competent and capable, than venturing beyond into unknown, scary territory alone. If we will get better at making it out of our safe zones, then we must surround ourselves with talented, capable, and ambitious female counterparts. If you frequently are in rooms where no one dreams bigger than you, then you need to be in a different room. You will not grow personally fast enough if you aren't challenged and inspired by the people you surround yourself with. Putting yourself on the path of inspiration is critical to your growth and critical in creating a sense of safety as you start playing a riskier game. Surrounding yourself with other women who are going further, running harder, and building bigger is a huge source of comfort and encouragement and a great stimulator for personal growth. It puts wind in your sails that pushes you on, causing hunger in your heart and potentially moving you from where you are today to where you could go or get to.

I remember the first time I ever went on an Ernst & Young (EY) Entrepreneurial Winning Women retreat. I met women who had already built and sold their businesses and were talking about building their second business, running for office, starting venture capital firms, and thinking much bigger than I was at the time. They had ambition, and not only financial ambition, but they were also talking about solving big problems and tackling the challenges of our time that have not yet been solved. I was inspired by their vision and determination to do more. It made me continuously think bigger about my vision.

Being in the EY Entrepreneurial Winning Women network inspired me to think about things I'd never even thought about. And bizarrely, it created even more impetus for me to work on my business and to move on to do things that were still to come. Prior to being in rooms with those women, I'd never really imagined selling my business, nor had I imagined building something of intrinsic value. Still, suddenly, I could see why I'd want to do that. I could see a reason for building wealth. There was still more I could contribute to the world, things I could do to help move the world forward. I was inspired and encouraged by the women I met to believe that I had more to do and experience like them. They made my world bigger, which helped me be inspired to dream even bigger than I was already thinking. They challenged me not to play it safe but to feel a sense of safety and belonging as part of an ambitious group of women with big dreams.

Are you moving in circles that challenge you? Are you networking with people who are ahead of you? What conferences, networks, or groups could you participate in that would inspire and encourage you, or help you not play it safe? Where can you connect with others who will inspire and challenge you? If you already know more or have the biggest dream in your group or network, you are in the wrong group! You need to be moving in spheres where people are ahead of you, know more than you, and where you can learn, be inspired, and grow. If you are going to beat the temptation to play it safe, you need to be encouraged and inspired, the flame within you being nurtured, challenged, and fanned into an even greater flame so that you might set the world on fire. Because remember, if not you, then who? The world needs you to bring your A game, to be all that you can be, and accomplish all you are capable of accomplishing. You owe it not only to your business and employees, but also to yourself and your family. Put yourself on the path of inspiration.

In the United States, there are several female-focused networks aimed at supporting female entrepreneurs. The EY Entrepreneurial Winning Program (https://www.ey.com/en_us/entrepreneurial-winning-women-north-america) I've mentioned is one of them. Dell Women's Entrepreneur Network, or DWEN (https://dwen.com/en-us/), is another. The Women Presidents Organization, or WPO (www.women-presidents.com), is a third. Then, of course, there are organizations like Entrepreneurs' Organization (EO; https://hub.eonetwork.org/) for both men and women and for early-stage female entrepreneurs (founders currently generating less than one million dollars), and there is the BrainTrust (ourbraintrust.org), which was founded by Sherry Deutschmann, whose story we heard earlier.

In addition to these networks, many of which are global organizations, there are myriads of networks for women entrepreneurs outside the United States. Africa Women Innovation and Entrepreneurship Forum (AWIEF; https://www.awieforum.org/), Future Females (https://join.futurefemales.co/), and Lionesses of Africa (https://www.lionessesofafrica.com/), to name a few, are all organizations in Africa focused on supporting female entrepreneurs. Similarly, numerous other regional organizations in Europe, Latin America, and the Asia–Pacific are fulfilling the same role. The key is to find a network you can be a part of that will help you think bigger and not allow you to play it safe.

Having strong networks can offer more than just a fresh perspective. The relationships built through your networks will also help you achieve tangible results. Imagine learning from the experiences of others, gaining access to the connections of others, and having doors opened for you. This only scratches the surface of the value networks provide.

During my interview process for the EY Entrepreneurial Winning Women network, I told the panel, "I am the least networked person out there. I need to join this community because I recognize I need the help of others." At the time, I didn't realize how valuable that group would be to me, and not just as inspiration, but also practically. If I needed input on how to do something, a connection, or to understand how someone had made something happen, all I had to do was ask. Suddenly, a door opened into a world that provided me with endless opportunities and wider connections. I built business relationships and friendships in a community that could help me do more business, help me move forward, and help me grow and learn quickly. Women have often misunderstood the value of networks. We've not fully appreciated how much business takes place on the golf course between people (often men) who have relationships with one another! But that is really what great networks are; being well networked is having great relationships, relationships that can help us do more business and through which we can help others do more. Without great relationships, it's difficult to succeed in business. So, the next time you are invited to a networking event, don't dismiss it as wasting your time and energy. Worry less about being transactional in your conversations and more about building connections and relationships because those people could help open doors for you for years. Who they know, as well as what they know, could be valuable to you.

Women Who Grow Believe in Themselves

Shortly after deciding to raise capital and drive exponential growth for our business, I regularly met with a business coach. I recognized that not only did we need capital, but I also needed to grow. We needed to invest in my leadership if we were going to make significant progress.

At first, this idea of meeting with a coach was not an easy pill to swallow because hiring their help wasn't cheap. I knew I needed someone who had exponentially grown revenue streams and built a big business before, so that expertise was expensive. I realized, though, that just like we had to invest in the business, we also had to invest in me leading that business, and therefore, getting a coach was just as significant as raising capital. If we want to go far, we must keep growing; we must keep learning the countless things we don't yet know and unravel the mindsets and beliefs that slow us down. I discovered that doing my own internal work with a coach and therapist was critical to my development. I have, therefore, long since believed that a company's growth is very much dependent on our personal growth. How fast your business can grow is greatly affected by how fast we, as founders, can learn and grow. Our personal growth, our ability to learn, evolve, discover, and transform, and the speed at which we do these things are directly connected to your business's growth and the speed of growth. In Chapter 3, we discussed how critical talented people are to creating successful enterprises. A rapidly growing enterprise needs founders who will evolve, grow, and develop themselves rapidly—not founders who are busy questioning and doubting whether they should or should not do something.

How fast are you growing into all that you need to be for your business to be a success? Could it be that if your business growth is stagnant or not growing as fast as you would like, you aren't growing fast enough? It's challenging to think that our personal development can have such a critical role in our success, as it requires us to take responsibility and action. Yet, at the same time, it is incredibly empowering to realize we can control and do something about our growth if we invest in ourselves.

Personal growth does not happen naturally or as a byproduct of getting older. We might have more experience, which might make us wiser in some ways, but that's different from personally growing. To distill our experiences into wisdom, we must transform our learnings into new patterns of behavior and action. In some ways, getting older can make us less prone to personal growth and more likely to be stuck in our outdated and unhelpful ways of thinking. It's not unusual to need help seeing what needs to change, what attitude must go, what way of being needs adjusting, what fears need addressing, and what knowledge gaps need to be filled. I have found enormous benefits from having a coach and therapist in my life for a long time. They both play different roles, but there is often overlap between the two different resources, because who I am and how I think both deeply affect my ability to grow my business and be the leader I want to be in the world. A business coach is there to ask you tough questions, help you see things you haven't seen before, and help you find solutions to problems that were in you all along but you did not realize or have the courage to execute. The lessons I have learned from my various coaches have bolstered my ability to make tough decisions, put necessary leadership building blocks in place, hire the top talent I needed to take my business to the next level, and stay focused on executing goals. Having someone in your life focused on helping you grow and identify your blind spots and mindsets holding you back is critical in helping you navigate and overcome your own personal limits and unhelpful behaviors while becoming increasingly more confident in who you are and where you are going.

Women Who Rest

One of the unintended side effects of the feminist movement has been the unrealistic expectations placed upon women to be able to "do it all." We asked for it all and must prove we can "do it all." The pressures to prove we are just as capable has thrust women into the trap of not only trying to climb the ladder successfully but also bearing the full burden of raising and caring for our children and families. The climb is often overwhelming, leaving women feeling burned out, unable to ask for help or support, and unable to rest. The pressures and stakes feel enormous. All too often, women fall deeply into the trap of believing "everything depends on me." In reality, we are only as capable as the care we take of ourselves. By putting our oxygen masks on first, we lead well and stop acting like foot soldiers taking heavy fire, scrambling to stay alive. We free ourselves to start acting like generals able to survey the big picture and gain perspective, allowing us to lead and make strategic calls.

I have found that a critical element to my personal growth and development has been carving out space and time from my normal surroundings and routine. This breathing space allows me to think and ask hard questions while reading, listening, and learning. By changing my surroundings and stepping momentarily away from my normal family responsibilities, I give myself a chance to see things differently, realize things I had not realized before, and gain the capacity to ponder. Stepping out has helped me solve some of the toughest challenges I have faced in business and has given me the renewed energy to keep going. Taking away the distractions of the busyness of everyday life and creating space for myself to get away and reflect on my bigger picture has been good for everyone around me and my business. Every time I have stepped away from my business and family for a few days (and I try to do this three times a year), I have had enormous clarity, refreshment, and a different perspective. When managing a busy household, caring for children, or simply sharing a life with a partner and running a business, it is so easy to get lost in what is right in front of us and lose our perspective and sense of direction. Carving out time always feels selfish or impossible because we think, "I've got kids, work, home, and responsibilities that no one else can pick up." But I genuinely believe this mindset of "it's all on me" stunts our personal lives, our business lives, and the lives of those around us. Suppose we do not make space for rest and reflection, and fail to lay down the superhero martyr within each of us. In that case, there is no way to empower and create space for others to step up, and there is no room for another's growth, which will keep us all living a small life that revolves around us being the manager and controller of everything. Women who go big don't do everything. They get help, they allow others in, and they recognize the world will not fall apart if they step out for a while. If it does, maybe it needed to be rebuilt anyway. There has never been a time after I've been away on a retreat or simply had a morning by myself that I've thought, "Gosh, everyone and everything in my life is going to be worse off because I've spent time alone!"

Rest and reflection enrich my life. Some of my biggest, most creative ideas and biggest deals have been done when my schedule is empty, and I'm exploring and out of my regular routines. More can be accomplished in one week or one day on retreat than a thousand years in your routine and rhythm, because we stop the busy work and do the real work of thinking big and solving our biggest challenges.

In April 2019, I traveled by plane to a conference across the country. I read an article headlined, "39 Million Americans Can't Afford a Vacation this Summer."[3] The enormity of that number and how wrong that felt stopped me in my tracks. The article explained that for many people, a vacation was a luxury they simply couldn't afford. Taking a break from work was an impossibility for financial reasons.

Knowing how critical my own special times vacationing with my family were and how important it was for my health and well-being, I had an idea. Our mission at Under Canvas was to help families connect with nature and reconnect with each other. So, it struck me we could help contribute to solving this same problem that 39 million Americans had. I called my team to pitch the idea within hours of landing. "What if we gave vacations away this summer?" There was silence on the other end of the phone. "I'm serious. What if we helped some of those 39 million Americans who aren't going to get a vacation this year get one!" The team picked their jaws up off the ground and considered the concept. I pitched the idea of having a "pay-what-you-can-campaign" to allow guests to fill out an online form and tell us what they *could* afford to pay for a summer vacation. Then, we could select families around the country with compelling stories and huge needs to vacation at Under Canvas that summer. We implemented the idea within a month, and the campaign went live. We ended up giving over one thousand vacations away. Some guests paid nothing, and others paid a few hundred dollars, a fraction of the normal cost, but everyone was extraordinarily thankful, and the kudos for our brand went through the roof.

Being out of the office, out of my routine, and getting headspace to do a simple thing like reading a magazine gave me one of my best ideas. From a marketing perspective, it was extraordinary, but even more importantly, we demonstrated our values to the world; nothing had ever spoken louder.

I have always believed that travel is transformative, but having the headspace and time to reflect, think, be, imagine, create, unravel, and rest is even more so. We are human beings, not human doings, and when we rest and give ourselves time and space, we can lean toward being, which will do ourselves and our businesses some good.

We do not need to buy into the mindset that says, "We have to do it all." Quite the contrary. We do ourselves, our families, and our businesses a disservice when we live like everything depends on us. Let's stop trying to be the martyrs no one needs us to be and carve out time to invest in ourselves and our businesses by regularly stepping out to get the fresh perspective we need. You never know; your next best idea might just come through while you're out relaxing. At the very least, taking the breathing space to rest and reflect refuels your capacity to persevere, giving you the strength to tackle tough obstacles and challenges.

Women Tackling Challenges

The entrepreneurial journey is one of the toughest paths out there. Being constantly bombarded by crises, challenges, obstacles, and life-and-death decisions for the business is exhausting and grueling on a level that's difficult to explain to those who have never done it. Growing a business is never a linear journey, yet when we view those challenges and obstacles as unexpected, terrible events, we throw ourselves emotionally off course. Our perception of challenges can hinder and drain us. Think about how much emotional energy you have spent this week alone worrying about a challenge or problem in your business. What if we could shift our perspective on problems and obstacles? Instead of being surprised when they surface or seeing them as enormous threats that cause crises and stress that steal our peace, what if we expected them and recognized these challenges as a normal part of our journey, showing us our path forward? Imagine what a shift in our own mental health that would make!

The very nature of growing a business is solving one problem after another after another, and each problem or obstacle represents a huge opportunity. Every time a problem or obstacle shows up, they inadvertently create an opportunity for a breakthrough. Like in a computer game, overcoming obstacles and challenges helps us reach the next level; we advance and move forward. Advancement does not come without solving the challenges or complexities of that level. If you have ever worried about your children playing too many computer games, as I have, remind yourself that they have been inadvertently learning how to level up!

We must get better at leveling up in life and business. When each of us reaches the end of our lives, what we managed to accomplish will be related to how we approached life's challenges. Whether we shun obstacles, ignore them, are afraid of them, or tackle them quickly and efficiently, learning everything we can from them, will determine whether we keep moving up to solve next-level challenges or not.

Instead of being fearful or overwhelmed by challenges, we've got to look at them and go, "How do I suck every last bit of growth out of this problem as fast as I possibly can so I can see my business grow more and move on to the next set of challenges." If I can see challenges as learning and growth opportunities, my approach to them will differ from seeing them as disastrous hindrances to my life.

I've always been quite dramatic, seeing everything in black and white, life and death terms. But imagine for a moment being delighted because you've got a problem. Ecstatic because you've been blessed with a ginormous challenge you don't know how to solve. Imagine calling your closest friend to proclaim, "I'm overjoyed. I've got such a complicated problem that needs solving!" It sounds ridiculous, doesn't it? But that's closer to the mindset we've got to develop if we want to have the stamina to grow and scale a business. We must start learning to love and embrace challenges as friends. They are a ladder or a bridge getting us to where our dreams want to take us. If we don't back off, give up, or get overwhelmed by our challenges, they will force us to become all we can be and do.

Every challenge has a way through, over, under, or around it. Whenever we discover the secret door to our breakthroughs, we have inadvertently grown in the process and allowed our business to move forward. Let me encourage you to start a new practice of being thankful for challenges, struggles, problems, and obstacles while remembering they are a sign that we are on the right path. In the end, our obstacles will guide us to the next level, provided we remain steadfast and do not shy away from our fear of the challenge at hand. The faster we overcome opposition, the faster we can move on to the next critical challenge. Let's be thankful for these growth opportunities.

Princess Leia flipped the damsel in distress stereotype entirely on its head. Dashing Han Solo, his trusty sidekick Chewbacca, and handsome young Luke Skywalker boldly ventured into the bowels of the massive Death Star to rescue the fair princess from the clutches of the evil Darth Vader. Little did they know, Leia would lead the rescue after the others had botched it. With Stormtroopers pouring in en masse, Leia shot out the garbage chute and ordered them to dive in. It may not have been the most glorious rescue, but it worked.

When you compete in big business, know that you will face an almost constant bombardment of problems, challenges, and obstacles designed to hold you back. Princess Leia's daring self-rescue reminds us of our ability to keep getting up, tackle the challenges before us, and not be surprised by them. Building a business is akin to navigating through a war zone. While you might achieve peace on one front, all hell may break loose on three other fronts. That's the constant ebb and flow of business. But if you intend to build an empire (or defeat one), you will have to fight many battles and take them in your stride without being rattled by them. The *Star Wars* battle was not won in a day. It consisted of strategic effort after effort until they had the map for the Death Star, and finally, they were in the perfect position to take it on, fly in, and shoot it out. Building a business is much the same. We'll have more fun if we can see each battle as a chance to advance. If we stay in the game and keep leveling up, we will build something extraordinary.

Women with No Limits

The only limit to what you can achieve is you. It doesn't matter where you've come from, how well-educated you are, what school you attended, or even how brilliant your business ideas are. What will cause you to rise or fall is between your ears, inside your own head. Reflecting on my journey, I have overcome enormous uncertainties, challenges, lack of capital, and lack of knowledge. Still, I believe a willingness to be adaptable, learn along the way, and recognize the mindsets that kept me stuck played a huge factor in my success.

It's never been easy for women to progress. The stats aren't getting any better, but putting ourselves in the way of inspiration, meeting other women on the same journey, getting a coach or mentor to walk alongside us, and taking time out to get perspective will all be critical components in helping you challenge your own mindsets and thinking. Our business growth depends on how fast we can grow personally. Investing in our growth is as critical as investing capital in our businesses.

What must you do to put yourself on a more rapid growth trajectory? What mindsets do you need to shed if you are going to build a business one hundred times bigger than you can imagine today? What kind of leader do you need to become to grow sufficiently to lead your business into its next season and era? How will you get the support to help you overcome your current challenges and help you keep overcoming challenge after challenge after challenge?

Your business needs you to level up to the next level. The world needs you to build an extraordinary enterprise that will create jobs, impact lives, drive change, and move the world forward. Please stop thinking small, playing safe, worrying about failing, questioning whether you should or could, fearing there is not enough, and believing you are not worthy of building and creating wealth. Stop thinking you can't or shouldn't or that there is no room at the table for you. Let's be thankful for every challenge that comes our way. Let's start believing that you can and will build something extraordinary. When you believe in yourself, others will, too.

Let's get out there. I'm rooting for you every step of the way.

Questions for Reflection

- What mindset is your greatest nemesis? What thoughts do you need to stop thinking and replace with better thoughts?
- What mindset shifts must you make to help you reframe and think differently?
- Who do you need to support you on your journey? What networks would be good to connect to?
- Can you plan some time into your schedule to help you change your perspective and see things differently?
- What is currently the biggest challenge or obstacle in your business? Are you spending 80 percent of your time and energy focused on solving that challenge so you can move on to the next problem?
- Can you be thankful today for the challenges and problems in your life and work?

Acknowledgments

There would be no story to tell, no wisdom to share, without the partnership of my incredible husband, Jake. This is our story and our journey, and I am so thankful for this crazy, wild ride we are on together. You have helped me think bigger than I could have ever dared to dream. Your brilliance, courage, determination, and constant encouragement to keep getting up have gotten me unstuck more times than I can count. Thank you for seeing me, and thank you for helping me become a better version of myself. Thank you for allowing me to tell our story and for being as passionate about helping other women succeed as I am. You are an incredible ally, an unsung hero who rarely gets the praise you deserve. We thank you for all that you do, all that you are, and for your genius, which you have allowed me to share on these pages.

To my amazing network and friends in the Ernst & Young Global Limited (EY) Entrepreneurial Winning Women Community: Thank you for being my tribe, the ones I call when I don't know what to do, when I need help, or when I need you to help someone else. Thank you. Thank you for showing me the way, enlarging my world, and making me believe that anything is possible. I said to Pat Headley in my interview to join this amazing crew, "I'm the least networked woman out there. I really need to join this network!" I really didn't realize just how badly I needed you all, but I do now. Thankfully, I am no longer alone, no longer unconnected, because I have you all. So many of you have shared your stories in this book, and you have given your time to help and support many of the women I support. Thank you for your constant generosity of spirit and for showing me what it looks like to hold your hands out toward other women.

To my Enygma Ventures investees: working with you all shaped this book. You enabled me to turn my story into one I hope will help many other women. Thank you for teaching me, challenging me, and giving me more companies (babies) to worry about! You have given me another life, a life I love. Your obstacles teach me new things every day as we seek to find solutions together. I feel privileged that we get to journey this path together.

To Lelemba Phiri and Sandras Phiri: you made our landing in Africa soft. You opened your world and your hearts to us. We would never have emotionally survived a global pandemic without your friendship, love, support, and encouragement to figure out this venture capitalist thing together. Without you both, there would have been no launch of Enygma. You opened a continent to us and keep inspiring us not to quit, even when no one else has caught on to the idea that investing in African women is a thing! Wakanda forever!

To my Mum and Dad, thank you for letting me go all those years ago when I first said, "I'm going to Africa." Thank you for the permission you've given me to follow my dreams and for giving me a safe place to return to when it all didn't go quite to plan. Thank you for believing in me, trusting me, and allowing me to be me. A parental safety net is a privilege many entrepreneurs don't have. You gave me that, which gave me the freedom to fail, freedom to try, and freedom to explore the world. I could not have gone on this journey without you. Thank you.

To my second Mom and Dad Dusek, you allowed us to come and invade the farm and live on your land, making it our home as well as yours. You gave us the opportunity to make magic happen. We know it wasn't always magical for you. We know we asked a lot of you. Thank you for giving us a shot and for allowing us to make our crazy ideas happen. Without you, there would be no Under Canvas today. What an extraordinary gift you gave to us all.

To everyone who worked at Under Canvas throughout the years, this is also your story. It is you, the extraordinary people who joined us on this journey, who brought Under Canvas to life, making it better and turning it into the company it is today. Thank you for your extreme resilience and tenacity, even when mine was failing. We know it looks easy to put tents up in a field, but you all know how hard it is! Your passion, dedication, and willingness to join two people with a crazy idea still humbles me. We still miss you all.

To my dear friends Rachel and Mike, you've walked with us on this journey from the very beginning. Mike, you hammered nails into walls, put up tents, designed our logos and marketing materials, and more. You helped us raise capital by designing incredible pitch decks, and you constantly say yes to me even when you have lots of other things on your plate. Rachel, you walk with me day in and day out. You tell me when I am crazy and when I'm not being crazy enough. Thank you for always helping me remember that there is always more! I consider it a privilege to do life with you.

To my friend Becky, we've solved big business crises, discussed strategy, cooked dinner, and folded laundry together all at the same time. Thank you for always being willing to lend me your ear, hear my anxieties, and walk with me on this unusual path. Your wisdom and your friendship are invaluable.

Milla, your invitation to visit you in Zimbabwe forever changed my life. You opened your world to me, and it forever changed mine. I will be forever thankful for all the ways Africa has shaped my life. Thank you!

Thank you, Robin Colucci, Sochil Washington, Mona de Vestel, and the whole team at Georgetown University Press, for helping me make this book a reality. Hilary Claggett, you said yes to a book for female entrepreneurs when few others were interested. Because of you, women around the world will get to see a pathway they can now pursue with confidence and clarity. Thank you for believing in women entrepreneurs and for believing in the importance of this book.

Thank you, finally, to you, my reader. I hope and pray that you find yourself in these pages and discover a roadmap that helps you bring your own unique greatness to the world. May you bring to life something even greater than you can imagine today. May you be inspired to think bigger than you ever have before. I can't wait to see what you are going to build.

Appendix: The Pitch Deck

SOLUTION

Tell us in one sentence your solution to the problem you've outlined.

PRODUCT

Showcase your Product:
Share video links, images, or diagrams to show off your products or services.

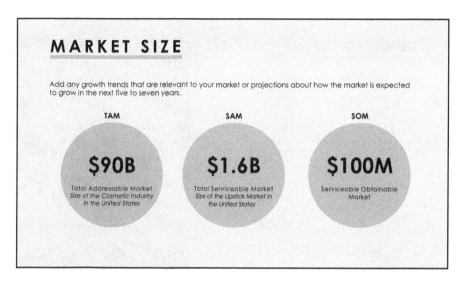

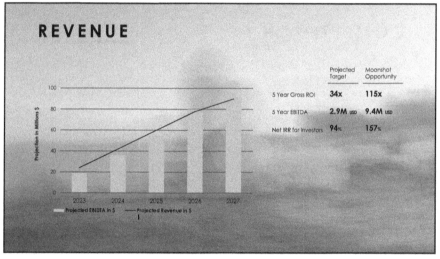

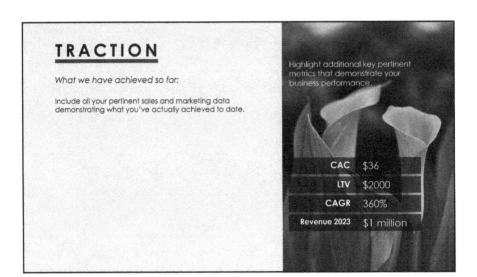

TRACTION

What we have achieved so far:

Include all your pertinent sales and marketing data demonstrating what you've actually achieved to date.

Highlight additional key pertinent metrics that demonstrate your business performance.

CAC	$36
LTV	$2000
CAGR	360%
Revenue 2023	$1 million

COMPETITION

	Quality 1	Quality 2	Quality 3	Quality 4
Your Company	●	●	●	●
Competitor Company	●	●		●
Competitor Company			●	●
Competitor Company		●	●	
Competitor Company	●			●
Competitor Company	●		●	
Competitor Company	●	●		●

TEAM

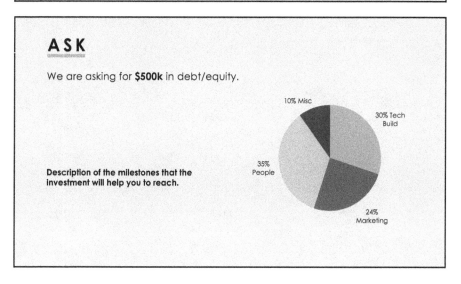

Name
Job Title
Brief relevant background
info

Name
Job Title
Brief relevant background
info

Name
Job Title
Brief relevant background
info

Name
Job Title
Brief relevant background
info

Name
Job Title
Brief relevant background
info

ASK

We are asking for **$500k** in debt/equity.

Description of the milestones that the investment will help you to reach.

10% Misc

30% Tech Build

35% People

24% Marketing

Additional Resources

Some of My Favorite Books

Acuff, Jon. *Soundtracks: The Surprising Solution to Overthinking (Overcome Toxic Thought Patterns and Take Control of Your Mindset).* Ada: Baker Books, 2021.

Bell, Rob. *How to Be Here.* New York: HarperOne, 2017.

Belsky, Scott. *The Messy Middle: Finding Your Way Through the Hardest and Most Crucial Part of Any Bold Venture.* New York: Portfolio, 2018.

Blank, Steve, and Bob Dorf. *The Startup Owner's Manual: The Step-by-Step Guide to Building a Great Company.* Hoboken: John Wiley & Sons, 2020.

Blanchard, Ken, and Colleen Barrett. *Lead with LUV: A Different Way to Create Real Success.* Upper Saddle River: Pearson PTR, 2010.

Brown, Brené. *Braving the Wilderness: The Quest for True Belonging and the Courage to Stand Alone.* New York: Random House, 2017.

Brown, Brené. *Rising Strong: How the Ability to Reset Transforms the Way We Live, Love, Parent, and Lead.* London: Vermilion, 2015.

Brown, Brené. *Daring Greatly: How the Courage to Be Vulnerable Transforms the Way We Live, Love, Parent, and Lead.* New York: Avery, 2015.

Christensen, Clayton M. *The Innovator's Dilemma: When New Technologies Cause Great Firms to Fail.* Boston: Harvard Business Review Press, 2016.

Collins, James C., and Morten T. Hansen. *Great by Choice: Uncertainty, Chaos, and Luck: Why Some Thrive Despite Them All.* New York: Harper Business, 2011.

Duckworth, Angela. *Grit: The Power of Passion and Perseverance.* New York: Scribner, 2016.

Gilbert, Elizabeth. *Big Magic: Creative Living Beyond Fear.* New York: Riverhead Books, 2015.

Goldin, Kara. *Undaunted: Overcoming Doubts and Doubters.* New York: HarperCollins Leadership, 2020.

Kern Lima, Jamie. *Believe IT: How to Go from Underestimated to Unstoppable.* New York: Gallery Books, 2021.

Lencioni, Patrick. *The Five Temptations of a CEO.* Hoboken: Jossey-Bass, 1998.

Miller, Donald. *Building a Story Brand: Clarify Your Message So Customers Will Listen.* New York: HarperCollins Leadership, 2017.

Moses, Mark. *Make Big Happen: How to Live, Work and Give Big.* Charleston: Forbes Books, 2016.

Moya-Jones, Raegan. *What It Takes: How I Built a $100 Million Business Against the Odds.* New York: Portfolio, 2019.

Sinek, Simon. *Start with Why: How Great Leaders Inspire Everyone to Take Action.* New York: Portfolio, 2009.

Sinek, Simon. *The Infinite Game.* New York: Portfolio, 2019.

Willink, Jocko, and Leif Babin. *Extreme Ownership: How U.S. Navy SEALS Lead and Win.* New York: St. Martin's Publishing Group, 2015.

Podcasts

Suneera Madhani, *CEO School*, https://theceoschool.com/the-podcast/

John Warrillow, *Built to Sell Radio*, https://builttosell.com/podcast/

Mark Moses and Steve Sanduski, *CEO Coaching International Podcast*, https://ceocoachinginternational.com/podcasts/

Guy Raz, *How I Built This*, https://wondery.com/shows/how-i-built-this/

Nikki Barua, *Beyond Barriers Podcast*, https://www.gobeyondbarriers.com/podcast/byob-podcasts/blog/turn-your-obstacles-into-opportunities-with-nikki-barua

Kara Goldin, *The Kara Goldin Show*, https://karagoldin.com/podcast/

Sarah Dusek, *Venture Forward*, https://www.youtube.com/channel/UCb4Qas6hGU8t723jFb6I4lw

Nathan Beckord, *How I Raised It: The Podcast Where We Interview Founders Who Have Raised Capital*, https://blog.foundersuite.com/tag/how-i-raised-it-podcast/

Nicole Jansen, *Leaders of Transformation Podcast*, https://leadersoftransformation.com/podcasts/

Notes

1. The Heart of the Problem

Epigraph: Marian Wright Edelman, "It's Hard to Be What You Can't See," *Huffington Post*, August 21, 2015, https://www.huffpost.com/entry/its-hard-to-be-what-you-c_b_8022776.

1. Amy Diehl, Leanne M. Dzubinski, and Amber L. Stephenson, "New Research Reveals the 30 Critiques Holding Women Back from Leadership That Most Men Will Never Hear," *Fast Company*, May 2, 2023, https://www.fastcompany.com/90889985/new-research-reveals-critiques-holding-women-back-from-leadership-that-most-men-will-never-hear.

2. Malin Malmstrom, Jeaneth Johansson, and Joakim Wincent, "We Recorded VC Conversations and Analyzed How Differently They Talk About Female Entrepreneurs," *Harvard Business Review*, May 17, 2017, https://hbr.org/2017/05/we-recorded-vcs-conversations-and-analyzed-how-differently-they-talk-about-female-entrepreneurs.

3. Grace LaConte, "Financial Facts About Women-Owned Business," *LaConte Consulting*, August 5, 2022, https://laconteconsulting.com/2022/08/05/financial-facts-women-business/.

4. Dominic-Madori Davis, "Women-Founded Startups Raised 1.9% of all VC funds in 2022, a drop from 2021," *TechCrunch*, January 18, 2023, https://techcrunch.com/2023/01/18/women-founded-startups-raised-1-9-of-all-vc-funds-in-2022-a-drop-from-2021/.

5. Going Public, "Fewer Than 30 Women Founders Have Ever Taken A Company Public," *Entrepreneur*, February 10, 2022, https://www.entrepreneur.com/business-news/fewer-than-30-women-founders-have-ever-taken-a-company/414759#:~:text=Fewer%20Than%2030%20Women%20Founders%20Have%20Ever%20Taken%20a%20Company%20Public%20%7C%20Entrepreneur.

2. Solutions Require Failure

Epigraph: John F. Kennedy, "Day of Affirmation Address," transcript of speech
delivered at the University of Capetown, Capetown, South Africa, June 6, 1966,
https://www.jfklibrary.org/learn/about-jfk/the-kennedy-family/robert-f-kennedy/
robert-f-kennedy-speeches/day-of-affirmation-address-university-of-capetown-
capetown-south-africa-june-6-1966.

1. James C. Collins and Morten T. Hansen, *Great by Choice: Uncertainty, Chaos,
   and Luck: Why Some Thrive Despite Them All* (New York: HarperCollins
   Publishers, 2011).
2. Uri Levine, "Fail Fast – The Journey of Failures," February 21, 2018, https://
   urilevine.com/fail-fast-the-journey-of-failures/.
3. Uri Levine, "Tips for Entrepreneurs Embarking on Their Journey," January 24,
   2021, https://www.youtube.com/watch?v=dhOwiH2ANaM.
4. Elizabeth Gilbert, *Big Magic: Creative Living Beyond a Life of Fear* (New York:
   Riverhead Books, 2015), 24.

3. The Product Is Also You

Epigraph: "Thomas Jefferson Encyclopaedia," The Jefferson Monticello, accessed
April 2, 2023, https://www.monticello.org/research-education/thomas-
jefferson-encyclopedia/if-you-want-something-you-have-never-had-spurious-
quotation/.

1. James Clear, "40 Years of Stanford Research Found That People With this one
   Quality Are More Likely to Succeed," accessed February 18, 2024, https://
   jamesclear.com/delayed-gratification.
2. Rob Bell, *How to Be Here* (New York: HarperCollins, 2017), 129.
3. Tara Sophia Mohr, "Why Women Don't Apply for Jobs Unless They're 100%
   Qualified," *Harvard Business Review*, August 25, 2014, https://hbr.org/2014/08/
   why-women-dont-apply-for-jobs-unless-theyre-100-qualified.
4. Grand View Research Staff, "Glamping Market Size, Share & Trends Analysis
   Report by Accommodation (Cabins & Pods, Tents, Yurts, Treehouses), by Age
   Group, by Region, and Segment Forecasts, 2023–2030," Grand View Research,
   accessed April 25, 2023, https://www.grandviewresearch.com/industry-analysis/
   glamping-market.
5. Rumzz Bajwa, "5 Reasons Why Women Are Better and More Successful
   Entrepreneurs Than Men," Addicted2Success, September 14, 2020, https://
   addicted2success.com/entrepreneur-profile/5-reasons-why-women-are-better-
   more-successful-entrepreneurs-than-men/.

4. Market Size Supersized

Epigraph: Bruce Wilkinson, David Kopp, and Heather Kopp, *The Dream Giver: Following Your God-Given Destiny* (New York: Multnomah, 2003), 84.

1. *Field of Dreams*, directed by Phil Alden Robinson (1989; Universal City, CA: Universal Pictures, 1989), DVD.
2. Richard Branson (@richardbranson), "Dream big. If your dreams don't scare you, they are too small," Twitter (now known as X), July 19, 2017, https://twitter.com/richardbranson/status/887678479797559297.
3. Kim Parker, "Despite Progress, Women Still Bear Heavier Load Than Men in Balancing Work and Family," *Pew Research Center*, March 10, 2015, https://www.pewresearch.org/fact-tank/2015/03/10/women-still-bear-heavier-load-than-men-balancing-work-family/.

5. Revenue and the Metrics That Matter

Epigraph: The Mandela Foundation, accessed October 13, 2023, https://www.nelsonmandela.org/publications/entry/nelson-mandela-by-himself-the-authorised-book-of-quotations.

6. Traction and Proof of Concept

Epigraph: Tony Bodoh (@TonyBodoh), "You don't just declare to the world, 'This is who we are,' and it magically happens. You have to prove it to yourself, to your customers and to your employees," X (formerly known as Twitter), July 29, 2023, https://twitter.com/TonyBodoh/status/1685398389150588928.

1. Steve Jobs, "Steve Jobs: 20 Best Quotes," *ABC News,* October 6, 2011, https://abcnews.go.com/Technology/steve-jobs-death-20-best-quotes/story?id=14681795.

7. The Competition

Epigraph: Jamie Kern Lima, Believe It, (New York: Gallery Books, 2021).

1. Clayton M. Christensen, *The Innovator's Dilemma: When New Technologies Cause Great Firms to Fail* (Boston: Harvard Business Review Press, 2016), 18.

8. Teams for Tomorrow

1. Sarah Brady, "82% of Workers Would Consider Quitting Their Jobs Because of a Bad Manager," *Value Penguin*, January 12, 2022, https://www.valuepenguin.com/news/majority-workers-would-leave-job-becuase-of-manager.

9. Asking for Funding and Getting It

Epigraph: John F. Kennedy, "President John F. Kennedy's Inaugural Address," transcript of speech delivered at the United States Capitol, Washington DC, January 20, 1961, https://www.archives.gov/milestone-documents/president-john-f-kennedys-inaugural-address.
1. Devishobha Chandramouli, "New Study Finds 5 Key Differences in How Male and Female Founders Raise Capital," *Entrepreneur*, April 10, 2018, https://www.entrepreneur.com/starting-a-business/new-study-finds-5-key-differences-in-how-male-and-female/311307.

10. The World Is Waiting for You

Epigraph: Malala Yousafzai, "16th Birthday Speech at the United Nations," transcript of speech delivered at the United Nations, New York, NY, July 12, 2013, https://malala.org/newsroom/malala-un-speech.
1. Brené Brown, *Rising Strong: How the Ability To Reset Transforms The Way We Live, Love, Parent, and Lead* (London, England: Vermilion, 2015), 47.
2. Ruth Bader Ginsburg, "When will there be enough women on the Supreme Court? Justice Ginsburg answers that question," interview by Gwen Ifill, Georgetown University, PBS News Hour, February 5, 2015, audio 1:23, https://www.pbs.org/newshour/show/justice-ginsburg-enough-women-supreme-court.
3. Gary Stroller, "39 Million Americans Can't Afford a Vacation This Summer," April 25, 2019, https://www.forbes.com/sites/garystoller/2019/04/25/39-million-americans-cant-afford-a-vacation-this-summer/?sh=6c723825107c.

Index

About the Author

Sarah Dusek is the cofounder of Enygma Ventures, a private investment fund dedicated to supporting and investing in women-led businesses in Africa. Since Enygma's inception in 2019, over 20,000 entrepreneurs have gone through Enygma's investor-ready programs to learn how to build valuable companies. Sarah aims to demystify the complicated and often inaccessible world of funding and make capital accessible for women, helping them to both deliver outstanding outcomes for their own businesses and drive economic and social progressive change.

In 2009, she founded, together with her husband Jake, the leading upscale outdoor hospitality brand Under Canvas, which she built into a company worth over $100 million in just six years. Under Canvas received a spot on the coveted Inc. 5000 list in 2017, and in the same year Sarah was also named to Ernst & Young's EY Entrepreneurial Winning Women list as a forward-thinker and changemaker.

In 2024, Sarah and Jake launched Few & Far, a new travel company connecting curious travelers to conservation initiatives around the world and the duo opened their first safari style lodge in South Africa. Sarah is a passionate traveler and wholeheartedly believes in the power of the outdoor hospitality industry to protect and preserve the world's wild places.

Sarah sits on the board of ten startup companies in Africa and divides her time between the US and Africa with her husband Jake and their two children. To connect with Sarah, visit www.sarahhdusek.com or www.enygmaventures. com for more information on getting funded.